G

A

CN00969450

EDWARD J. YOUNG

GENESIS 3

A devotional & expository study

EDWARD J. YOUNG

THE BANNER OF TRUTH TRUST

THE BANNER OF TRUTH TRUST
3 *Murrayfield Road, Edinburgh EH12 6EL*
PO Box 621, Carlisle, Pennsylvania 17013, USA

*

© THE BANNER OF TRUTH TRUST 1966
FIRST PUBLISHED 1966
REPRINTED 1983
ISBN 0 85151 148 1

*

Set in 11 on 13 point Garamond
and printed and bound in Great Britain by
McCorquodale (Scotland) Ltd., Glasgow

Prologue

GENESIS THREE is a part of the Holy Scripture and in the brief study which follows we have so understood it. Today there is much written about the human origin of the Bible, and the third chapter of Genesis has not escaped attention. Endeavours have been made to discover the 'traditions' which supposedly are mirrored or reflected in this chapter. Attempts are made to tie it up in one way or another with extra-Biblical literature of antiquity.

We have had occasion to mention some, but not all of these attempts, for our primary purpose is not to refute the various theories concerning the origin of the chapter which are today in vogue but to seek, as best we are able, to present what we believe to be the meaning of the chapter. There is a desperate need today for a study of the content of the Bible. Too much time is devoted to questions concerning the type of literature found in the Bible, to the history of oral and written transmission and the like, but all too little endeavour is given to a serious consideration of the content of the Holy Bible.

And the Scriptures are the Holy Bible. In this third

chapter of Genesis we are not dealing with human traditions, but with the revealed Word of the ever living God. How God revealed the contents of this chapter to man we do not know, nor is it our purpose to consider how Moses, whom we believe to be the human writer of the chapter, received the information contained herein. Our earnest prayer is that the modern reader, with the help of these pages, will come to a deeper understanding of what Genesis Three teaches. May he realize the depth to which Adam plunged the human race, but may he also realize how great was the love of God that sent a second Adam whose atoning work has paid the debt of man's sin.

It is a pleasure to express my gratitude and indebtedness to Mrs. Charles L. Eckardt for the careful manner in which she prepared the typescript.

1. Now the serpent was more subtil than any beast of the field which the LORD God had made. And he said unto the woman, Yea, hath God said, Ye shall not eat of every tree of the garden?

*N*ow the serpent! With these words this chapter begins. Moses has placed them at the head of the chapter for emphasis. All the stress falls on them. We are not told what kind of a serpent it was, nor do we know how large or small it was. Such considerations are not important. What is important is that we are dealing with a serpent, or, if you will, a snake.

But is not the snake really Satan? Or is not the snake Satan's instrument? Some commentaries begin by saying that the snake is not an embodiment of a demonic power or of Satan. They are very positive about this. Are they right? These are questions which cannot be dismissed, but this is not the place to answer them. It is better to follow the procedure of the Bible itself and to look into such questions at the proper time. For the time being what we must insist upon is that the chapter immediately confronts us with a snake.

If there were no snake but merely an appearance, we might very well question the historicity of the narrative, for if the Bible spoke of a snake but did not mean a snake, we might justifiably wonder whether it did not do the same thing with other objects mentioned in this chapter. If the word 'snake' is simply a symbol for something else, how do we know that other things which we meet in this chapter are not also mere symbols? It is not amiss then to lay our stress upon this first word, and to insist that the chapter begins by directing our attention to a real snake.

Moses does this in an interesting manner. Were we to translate the Hebrew literally, we should read 'and the snake'. The King James version brings out the force well in English when it renders, 'now the serpent.' Thus, at the very beginning, the serpent is thrust, as it were, before our eyes.

Not only is the serpent a beast, however, he is also a creature of God, for we are told that he was more subtle than any beast of the field which the Lord God had made. What is meant is that God made all the beasts of the field, and of all these beasts the serpent was the most subtle. Inasmuch as God made the snake, the snake was good. It was not some power that existed independently of God, but owed its very being to Him.

Of all the creatures which the LORD God had made, the snake, says the Scripture, was the most subtle. Yet this is a difficult conception. How can we say that a snake is subtle? Wherein does that subtlety consist? Our Lord may have had reference to this description when in sending forth His disciples, He said to them, 'Behold, I send you forth as sheep in the midst of wolves: be ye therefore wise as serpents, and harmless as doves.' (Matthew 10:16)

The Hebrew word which is translated 'subtil' is pronounced *aroom*. It is spelled almost identically with the word *arom* which in Genesis 2:25 is translated 'naked'. There would seem then to be some connection between nakedness and subtlety. Perhaps the word 'subtil' suggests slyness and cunning. The snake was crafty. Its wisdom was not something good but something evil. Snakes possess a certain fascination which has led the writer of the Proverbs to exclaim: 'There be three things which are too wonderful for me, yea, four which I know not: The way of an eagle in the air; the way of a serpent upon a rock; the way of a ship in the midst of the sea; and the way of a man with a maid' (Proverbs 30:18, 19). It is true that the gliding of the snake across the rock causes astonishment. We watch the serpent and are spellbound. Is this, however, what is meant by a snake's subtlety? It would hardly seem so, for the way of a serpent upon the rock, like the other actions mentioned in the Proverb, is amoral and leaves no visible trace.

The word 'subtil' is evidently used with respect to what follows, where the words spoken by the serpent tempt the woman and lead her into moral evil. It is this fact which throws the true light upon the meaning. And in the light of this fact it would seem that the subtlety is something which could belong only to a responsible being. No mere snake could of itself display the craftiness and cunning which manifest themselves in the subsequent discourse with Eve. When therefore the Bible asserts that the serpent is subtle it is taking the first step, it would seem, in going behind the scene and letting us know that there is more here than meets the eye. A subtlety is at work such as does not belong to snakes. That much, it appears, we must grant, if we are to do justice to what the Bible says. The word 'subtil' is the first hint that we have to deal with more than a snake.

At the same time there must also have been something in the snake which would make it possible to describe him as subtle. Some of his natural characteristics would evidently make him a suitable vehicle for the use of a power that could deceive mankind. What these character-istics were we do not know, and there is little profit in trying to speak where Scripture is silent. The snake, we read, is the most subtle of all beasts, and yet the subtlety which manifests itself is such that it can be the possession of no mere snake alone; its presence hints at a being higher than the snake.

It is this snake which speaks. On that point there can be no doubt, for the Scripture plainly states: 'And he (i.e. the snake) said to the woman.' Snakes however, if we may state the obvious, do not speak. What then are we to do with this statement of Scripture? There are some who find no problem at all. The important thing, they tell us, is not whether a snake spoke or not, but what it said. 'Let us examine carefully the words of the serpent, and not be concerned as to whether he spoke them or not.' With this interpretation, however, we cannot rest satisfied. Were we reading some harmless fable, such as those of Lokman or Aesop, we would not be concerned about the speaking of an animal, for in fables we expect animals to speak. Their speaking is harmless and enter-taining and we think nothing of it. What the animals say in a fable is obviously the important thing.

With Genesis Three, however, the situation is different, or is it? Do we have in Genesis Three just another fable?

That is the way in which some have explained the chapter. Here, they say, is an animal which speaks, and inasmuch as speaking animals are characteristic of fables, we have such a fable here in the first book of the Bible.

With such an interpretation we cannot for a moment agree. When we compare Genesis with well-known fables we immediately perceive that there is a tremendous difference between them. In fables animals do talk, and as just remarked, that is what we expect. The wolf, drinking upstream from the lamb, complains to the lamb that the lamb is muddying the water. Our thoughts turn immediately to the cruelty and injustice of the charge, and we know only too well that it is but a pretext on the wolf's part so that he may devour the lamb. A moral is appended, and the moral calls to mind those who act as did the wolf. We recoil from the cruelty of those who are stronger than the weak and who for their own satisfaction take advantage of the weak. Here it is the moral which really engages our attention and we pay little or no attention to the fact that animals are presented to us as speaking. Indeed, most fables are quite useful in that they do teach a lesson. We could do far worse than to spend our time in the reading of some of the classic fable writers.

Genesis Three, however, strikes one immediately in that it differs so markedly from the ordinary fable. For one thing, it has no moral attached to it, as is the case with the fables of Propertius or Aesop or Lokman. Evidently Genesis is not teaching us a moral as the classical fables seek to do. Then too, whether we are willing to acknowledge it or not, we cannot help but be somewhat struck by the fact that in Genesis a serpent speaks. This is unusual; it is not what we expect. We read of speaking animals in the fables and are not disturbed thereby. We read Genesis, however, and are disturbed. The speaking serpent is out of order. It is something which we had not expected.

There is a seriousness about these early chapters of Genesis which is not to be found among the writers of fables. That the wolf ate the lamb is a sad story, but we know that in this particular case it never happened. We simply cannot take the fables seriously. We may indeed take seriously the morals which they teach, but as to the actual fables themselves, we do not regard them as accounts of events which actually transpired. In reading Genesis, however, we find ourselves in a different attitude. This account demands to be taken seriously and we read it to hear what it has to say. The result of the serpent's speaking is that mankind became plunged into misery, and we realize that we are dealing with something that cannot be lightly brushed aside as is the case with a fable.

Not all who study Genesis, however, seem to appreciate the seriousness which characterizes it. An ancient Jewish tradition, which appears in the Talmud, tells us that the serpent is simply a symbol of the evil impulses that are found in the human heart. Again, it has been suggested that we should not be too concerned at discovering that a serpent speaks, for in Paradise everything is miraculous and of a higher order from what we know. In such a wonderful place why should it be surprising to find that one of the animals which God had created engages in speech?

A little reflection, however, will show that such interpretations are not admissible. We shall return in a moment to the interpretation presented in the Talmud. With respect to the idea that the Paradise was a place of marvel and wonder in which we should not be surprised to find a snake speaking, the following may be noted. This interpretation practically makes of the account a fairy tale. It sees Paradise as a place of wonderful people and animals who can do the things that we ordinary men and women are unable to do. But this is not the picture that Genesis gives. It does not bring us into some mysterious fairyland of wonderful animals and peoples, some never-never land of the children's story books. Instead, we behold the Paradise of God, the garden which He in loving care prepared for man's dwelling. And in the present chapter we have found a jarring, discordant note. In that wondrous paradise, where all is peace and where the glory of God covers the whole scene, a note of rebellion is sounded. A creature of God utters words of revolt. To dismiss this by saying that in this wonderland we should expect animals to speak or at least not be surprised if they do, is completely to misinterpret the nature of the narrative with which we are dealing.

What about the ancient Jewish view that the serpent was really a symbol of man's evil impulses? In recent times there has appeared a view quite similar to it which maintains that the serpent was a symbol of evil and that the concept rests upon an ancient tradition current among the Hebrews of Old Testament times. The serpent was thought to be connected with the sea, and the sea was conceived as a symbol of the forces of wickedness. This concept is based upon the idea that ultimately the sea was believed to have been in rebellion against the Creator. All such tradition, of course, is said to be no longer present in Genesis, but merely the serpent who symbolizes the power of evil.

According to this view there never was an actual serpent that spoke to the woman; the serpent possessed no objective existence. He was not there, perceivable to Eve's eyes, to address her and to tempt her into dis-obedience. What we read in Genesis is really simply an account of what occurred in the mind of the woman. This dialogue between the snake and the woman was not a conversation between two beings, but simply the woman's reasoning with temptation within herself, and the whole is clothed in the garb of a parable. The woman never saw any snake nor did she hold converse with one. She rather somehow fell into temptation and wrestled within herself as to what she should do. The account of that inward spiritual wrestling is given to us in the form of a dialogue between the serpent, who plays the role of the tempter, and woman herself. Evil triumphs; the temp-tation welling up within her mind becomes too strong, and she yields thereto.

Quite an ingenious interpretation! Does it not remove the difficulties occasioned by a strictly prosaic explana-tion? Well, for our part, we do not think that it relieves those difficulties at all. On the contrary, it even adds to them. If the serpent was not there present, but was nothing more than a symbol of evil, why is such a strong curse pronounced upon it? In verse fourteen the Lord speaks in vigorous tones of condemnation, and as a result the serpent is to go on his belly and eat dust, a sign of great degradation. What is the purpose of such language, if there was no serpent at all? Furthermore, why speak of enmity between the serpent and woman and of bruising the serpent's head, if there was no serpent present? The unusually vigorous condemnation pronounced by God in verses fourteen and fifteen seems almost pointless if the whole account is merely the story of an inward spiritual struggle on the part of Eve.

There is something else that needs to be noted. If the whole is nothing more than an account of Eve's struggle with temptation, we may well ask, how did she come to entertain these evil thoughts in the first place? It is true that in the condition in which she had been created, there was a possibility of her sinning, but we must distinguish between the possibility and the realization of that possibility. What caused her to realize that possibility? What became the occasion for evil thoughts to enter her mind? No, everything in the account suggests that a snake was actually present in the garden, and that this snake spoke to the woman. We cannot accept this modern interpretation, for it creates more difficulties than it resolves and it is not faithful to the sacred text. It is an attempt to escape some of the problems which arise from a straightforward realistic interpretation of the text, but it is not derived from the Scripture itself. A speaking serpent? That is a difficult conception, and in this context points to something deeper than appears upon the surface. It has been suggested that the language suggests the presence of the devil in the form of a serpent! If we read the language carefully we note that it does not say, 'Now the serpent was more subtil than any other beast of the field,' but simply, 'Now the serpent was more subtil than any beast of the field.' The argument is that the beasts of the field were subtle, but the serpent, which was not a beast of the field, was more subtle than any of them. Hence, the conclusion is derived that the word 'serpent' denotes something other than a mere snake.

Refined reasoning indeed! Refined, but, we fear, false. For if we look carefully at the opening words of the verse we read, 'now the serpent.' It is the little word 'the' which compels attention. This is the definite article, and in the Hebrew language the definite article is used in such a case to denote the genus. What the writer means then is simply that that species of animal known as 'serpent' was the animal which spoke to the woman.

Furthermore, to say that the serpent was more subtle than the beasts of the field does not necessarily imply that the serpent was not included in the category 'beasts of the field.' Rather, it would seem that the serpent was to be included in this category, for in verse fourteen it is condemned to go upon its belly. If the reference is to the devil or to some power higher than a snake, why this condemnation in verse fourteen? The snake belonged to the realm of earthly creatures, for it was soon to be brought into a particular relationship with man, the highest of these earthly creatures. Among other things, this chapter shows that, because of sin, the relationship between man, the crown of creation, and the lower creatures of earth, was broken.

In the snake therefore the animal world approached man; the animal non-material life approached the spiritual life of man. And the serpent spoke. At last we can look more closely at this thought. That the snake spoke shows without question that something is out of order; the snake was usurping to itself a prerogative which it did not rightfully possess.

When God created man, He brought before him all the animals and Adam gave them names. This statement, of course, has been the object of a great deal of ridicule. The present writer once read this passage with a professor of Hebrew who delighted in attempting to make Genesis look ridiculous. Here, he said, was the great parade. God placed Adam on a rock somewhere and then all the animals paraded before him, and as they passed, he pointed them out, 'There is a lion, there goes a tiger,' and so on, until he had completed his task. If, however, we pay some attention to what Genesis teaches, we shall make the discovery that, far from giving us a ridiculous picture, it presents us with something very profound.

When the Bible says that Adam gave names to the animals it means far more than that he merely looked at an animal and uttered some sound, possibly onomatopoeic in nature. In the Semitic languages to name something means to recognize and to mark out its essential nature and characteristics. When therefore Adam named the animals, he was classifying and categorizing. Inasmuch as he was created in the image of God and consequently possessed the faculty both of thought and speech he was able to name the animals. He knew what they existed for and what their relationship to him was. They could not name him, for they possessed neither the faculty of thought nor the gift of speech. In naming the animals Adam showed how utterly separate and completely different he was from them. Quite possibly he did utter some vocable by means of which he could designate and distinguish them, but whether that be so or not, this task of naming the animals demanded an exercise of intelligence upon his part such as the animals themselves did not possess.

In passing we may note that if there is any difficulty connected with Adam's naming the animals, we do not escape this difficulty by adopting some theory of evolution to account for the origin of man. If man evolved from something that was lower than himself—and anything that is non-man is considerably lower than man— then as soon as the first specimen of non-man became man—and in the nature of the case, the change had to be instantaneous—that man was confronted with the lower creation. Being a man he had to recognize the lower creation for what it was. Being a man, he possessed the ability to classify and to categorize the animals, whereas they could not so respond to him. The problem confronts us, no matter how we account for the origin of man. It is the height of folly, as well as being morally wicked, to attempt to make the divine revelation appear ridiculous at this point.

In Genesis, a serpent speaks. This serpent was one of the creatures which the Lord God had made. In that word 'made' we perhaps find a reflection upon the statement in the first chapter that God made the beast of the earth after his kind (1:25). The actions of the serpent, however, constitute a denial that God has made him. The serpent speaks; it does what animals cannot do. Only man, of earthly creatures, possesses the ability to speak.

Yet the serpent acts as a man; it raises itself above the beasts of the field which the Lord God had made and it elevates itself to an equality with man. There is something wrong and Eve should have recognized this as soon as the serpent began to speak.

Why does the serpent approach Eve rather than Adam? This is a difficult question to answer, and it is well not to be dogmatic where dogmatism is out of place. There are, however, certain Scriptural statements which should be noted. In writing to Timothy Paul says, 'For Adam was first formed, then Eve. And Adam was not deceived, but the woman being deceived was in the transgression' (1 Timothy 2;13, 14). Again Paul speaks of the serpent beguiling Eve through his subtlety (2 Corinthians 11:3) and in 1 Peter 3:7 the wife is spoken of as the weaker vessel. Eve was created in order to be a help to the man. Perhaps in this fact that she was the weaker vessel, that she was in a certain sense subordinate to man, being designed to be his help, the serpent found her more suitable to approach. She was the complement to man, and her presence was necessary in order that his existence might be whole and complete. Whether this lay in the fact that the woman, as has been suggested, was more sensitive and deeper in her soul toward nature, we cannot say. At any rate, the serpent approached her and in this approach manifests his subtlety. There was that in the being of the woman which made her a more suitable vessel to approach than the man. More than that it does not seem we are permitted to say.

At the same time we must note that sin serves to overthrow the order of things that God has instituted. She whom God in love had given to the man to be his help now becomes the instrument of his downfall. She does not prove to be a help but a hindrance. She does not encourage him to obedience to God but instead gives to him of the forbidden fruit.

How long a time had elapsed since man was placed in the garden and the approach of the serpent we do not know. An ancient Jewish tradition makes it seven years, but this is nothing more than tradition. How long the period of bliss existed, we cannot say, nor is it particularly important for us to know. What is important is that man lived in the garden with his help, Eve, and that he had named the animals. Here, without sin, he lived to the glory of God, until the serpent spoke to the woman.

With the serpent's first utterance it becomes apparent that an enemy of God is speaking. Those who are willing to dismiss this language as the mere language of animals, and to declare that in Paradise mankind has an understanding of the animals' tongue, have shown that they have not penetrated to the depth or heart of the matter. The first words uttered form a question, which seems designed to cast doubt upon God's goodness and yet, at the same time, seems to imply that if the serpent is misinformed, he is willing to be instructed in the matter. Perhaps we can to a certain extent bring out the force of the question if we render, 'Is it really a fact that God has prohibited you from eating of all the trees of the garden?'

Emphasis falls upon the word 'really.' 'God has created the garden and given it to you,' so the serpent seems to be saying. 'All these beautiful trees are at hand. Do you mean to say that God has said that you are not to eat from all of them.' It is a sly question, for whatever else it may do, it serves to implant within the mind the idea that God is unduly strict in not permitting Adam and Eve to eat from all the trees. 'Really? Can it possibly be?' One can almost hear the tone of voice as those words of wickedness are uttered.

The serpent is very careful to slip in the little word 'all,' for thereby he can cast doubt upon God's goodness; 'All these trees,' his thought appears to be, 'and you cannot eat from even one of them. God is keeping all of them to Himself.' At the same time, inasmuch as the language is phrased as a question, there seems to be present the suggestion that the serpent is willing to be corrected and instructed, if he is mistaken. Of course he has no desire to arrive at the truth. It is the impression which his question leaves that shows his subtlety. To Eve it would appear that here is a being asking a normal question and willing to be corrected and put right, if he is in error. As a matter of actual fact, of course, the serpent was simply giving a false impression. His question then was sly, but it was also false.

This raises a problem. A serpent speaks, but the serpent, a non-moral creature, suggests thoughts that are of a moral nature. The words of the serpent are morally wicked, but how can thoughts of a moral nature arise in a creature which does not have the capacity for moral distinctions? A snake is a mere snake; it does not know the difference between right and wrong. It has no mind which can distinguish right from wrong. How then can a mere snake, which is not a moral creature, make moral distinctions, as this snake is doing?

That a snake speaks is not to be doubted. All the evidence of Scripture shows that such was the case. At the same time, as soon as we read that a snake speaks we realize that there is more here than at first sight meets the eye. And when we note what the snake says, we know that here speaks forth the voice of the most deep-seated wickedness. It will not do to say, as some of the negative critics have done, that the Old Testament knows nothing of the devil until the time of the exile. This is an unjust statement. The fact that a certain document does not mention a particular subject does not mean that the author of the document does not know about the subject. It is just possible that he for some reason or other does not wish to mention that subject. Hence, merely because the devil is not expressly mentioned at this particular place does not mean that the human author of Genesis knew nothing of the devil.

In the Scriptures we discover a gradual progression with respect to revelation. God does not reveal the entire truth all at once. Rather, He imparts the truth bit by bit until His revelation is completed. This is so, for example, with the doctrine of the Trinity. In the Old Testament we do not find this doctrine fully presented to us as in the New Testament. We do find in the Old Testament, however, that certain glimpses of the doctrine are given, and these prepare us for the full revelation which occurs in the New Testament.

The case is similar with respect to Satan. In the verse before us the word Satan is not used. Nevertheless, it is perfectly clear that Satan is here at work. In the light of the plain statements of the New Testament we have every right to say that Eve was tempted of the devil. The evil thoughts which issued from the mouth of an actual snake found their origin in the devil himself.

In some sense that we cannot understand, for God has not revealed it unto us, the snake was an instrument used of the devil. To attempt to explain how the devil employ-ed the snake is a task of which we are not capable, nor is it particularly profitable that we should know how this was done. That it was done, however, the data of the Bible compel us to believe. We are far from saying that Eve herself understood this when the words issued from the serpent's mouth; even Moses, the writer of Genesis, may not have had the full knowledge of the subject that is possessed by New Testament believers. Speaking to the Pharisees our Lord said, 'Ye are of your father the devil, and the lusts of your father ye will do. He was a murderer from the beginning, and abode not in the truth, because there is no truth in him. When he speaketh a lie, he speaketh of his own; for he is a liar and the father of it' (John 8:44). And John speaks in the Revelation, 'And the great dragon was cast out, that old serpent, called the Devil, and Satan, which deceiveth the whole world; he was cast out into the earth, and his angels were cast out with him' (12:9); and again, 'And he laid hold on the dragon, that old serpent, which is the Devil, and Satan, and bound him a thousand years' (20:2). We are on good Scriptural ground, then, when we say that Satan used the serpent in order to tempt Eve.

One final thought. In the question of the serpent there is a glaring omission. The serpent asked, 'Has God said?' Studiously he avoids pronouncing the holy name by which the true God approaches His people. He does not say 'LORD.' Throughout chapter two we meet the combination 'LORD God,' but here we find only the word 'God.' Well did Satan know what he was doing. Oh! that those who do name the holy Name, the LORD, would also know what he is doing!

2. *And the woman said unto the serpent, We may eat of the fruit of the trees of the garden:*

*I*NSTEAD of turning away from the serpent the woman engages in dialogue with him, thereby revealing that she did not really realize that the serpent was her enemy and that she did not perceive his evil intentions toward her and her well-being. The serpent had approached the woman as one who had her best interests at heart, and this appearance was a deception. When the Lord Jesus Christ was tempted of the devil He knew His opponent. He engaged in no dialogue with him, but reproached him with the infallible words of Scripture. Eve should have done the same thing. She had no right to regard the serpent as one with whom she could profitably enter into discussion, for she knew full well the command of God.

There is a danger that today those who name the Name of Christ will be willing to meet error as though it were upon a par with the truth. As Christians we should ever be ready and prepared to give a reason for the hope that is within us, but we should never consider our Christian faith as only one of so many choices or options. We should not, for example, be willing to enter into what is called 'dialogue' with Roman Catholicism, as though we might mutually enrich one another by such discussion. Rather, if we have a true love for the Roman Catholic, we should in humility and love point out to him that what his church teaches is contrary to the revealed Word of God. All too often however, we approach evil, be it in life or in doctrine, in the same spirit in which Eve turned to the serpent. Instead of uttering, 'Thus saith the Lord,' we engage in dialogue and we do so at the peril of our own souls.

To speak to the serpent and to enter into discussion with him was wrong, for Eve should immediately have recognized, as soon as the Tempter spoke, that something was out of order. She knew full well that animals do not speak, and doubtless she had learned from Adam that he had named the animals. We may warrantably assume that she understood the implications of man's superiority over the beasts. Like Adam she possessed the ability to classify and categorize these animals and she knew that she herself was a help to Adam such as none of the animals could be.

Here, however, an animal was speaking; it was doing what an animal supposedly could not do. It was thus raising itself up above the domain of the lower creation and placing itself upon a par with man. More than that, in the content uttered it was apparent that the serpent was placing itself upon a par with, indeed, even above God. Absolute obedience upon Eve's part would have required that she forthwith denounce such sinful arrogance. In the words of the animal she should have perceived the voice of wickedness, that arrogant wickedness which would challenge the wisdom of the Divine commands. Had there been true love in the heart of Eve she would have risen to the defence of her Creator and denounced the wickedness of the one who insinuated that the Creator was not wise in His commands. Eve, however, was a modern and she followed the 'modern' practice of engaging in dialogue with the enemy of man.

In the first part of her reply, the part recorded in this second verse, she speaks the truth. 'Of the fruit of the trees of the garden we may eat,' she declares, and thus prepares to explain to the serpent the one exception to this rule which God had made. At the same time she does not stress the freedom to eat, as God had done in granting this freedom. He had said, 'From all the trees of the garden eating thou mayest eat.' (Genesis 2:16b). In granting this permission God's liberality had been manifested. God uses the word 'all' to make it clear that the entire garden was for man. In her reply to the serpent, Eve omits the word. Furthermore, God had stressed the fact that the eating was to be abundant, 'eating thou mayest eat,' He had said, and this idiom simply means that Adam might freely and abundantly partake of the fruit of all the garden's trees. Eve, however, does not emphasize this aspect of the matter and dismisses it with a mere 'we may eat.' When we engage in dialogue with evil we are very likely to give an incorrect impression of the truth.

3. But from the fruit of the tree which is in the midst of the garden, God has said, Not shall ye eat from it and not shall ye touch it, lest ye die.

*E*VE explains to the serpent concerning the tree whose fruit had been forbidden, describing it as being in the midst of the garden. God had not described its location, but had merely characterized it as the tree of the knowledge of good and evil. There is no necessary contradiction, for Eve, as we may well understand, is stressing the location of the tree and not its significance. The two clauses really complement one another. In Genesis 2:9 the tree of life was said to be in the midst of the garden. At this point, however, there is no need to mention the tree of life, and it certainly is unwarranted to say, as some commentators do, that at this point the narrative does not seem to know the tree of life. In replying to the serpent there would have been no reason to mention the tree of life. At the proper time the Bible does speak again about the tree of life, but that time has not yet come.

Why did Eve identify the tree as being in the midst of the garden and not as the tree of the knowledge of good and evil? It may be that she placed emphasis upon the site of location of the tree in the midst of the garden because its central location may have lent to it an aura of desirability. She uses the definite article, '*the* tree which is in the midst of the garden.' God had prohibited her and her husband from partaking of that particular tree. To her the forbidden tree was *the* tree, beside which the other trees lost their significance.

Some have attempted to discover a contradiction between what is stated here about the tree and the expressions of chapter two. In chapter two verse nine we are told that the tree of life is in the midst of the garden, and then the words 'and the tree of the knowledge of good and evil' are added. Here, however, Eve speaks of the tree of the knowledge of good and evil as being in the midst of the garden. Is there, however, really a contradiction? We do not think so. We have already noted why Eve speaks of the tree as being in the midst of the garden. In chapter two, however, the writer's desire evidently is merely to call attention to the presence of the tree. Why may we not simply assume that it and the tree of life were both in the midst of the garden? To expect a pedantic repetition of all the details of description every time there is mention of the tree is to expect the Scripture to become stiff and wooden.

Others have sought to avoid the difficulty by assuming that the tree of life and the tree of the knowledge of good and evil were one and the same. They arrive at this position by translating, 'and the tree of life in the midst of the garden, even the tree of the knowledge of good and evil.' This is a perfectly permissible and acceptable translation of the Hebrew, but, whereas it apparently delivers us from the supposed difficulty of reconciling what Eve says about the tree with what is stated in chapter two, it throws us into far greater difficulty. For, after man has eaten of the tree of the knowledge of good and evil, God drives him from the garden, lest he eat also of the tree of life. If the two trees are the same, then this action of the Lord is without meaning. Why should there be fear that man eat of the tree of life if he has already eaten from the tree and received death thereby? Here the writer simply brings out those details which at the time are significant for his purpose.

Eve's representation of God's command was to say the least not accurate. For one thing she makes the command general, placing it in the plural. God had commanded, 'Thou shalt not eat from it,' whereas Eve says, 'Ye shall not eat from it.' To this she also adds the words 'and ye shall not touch it.' By this addition she evidently was attempting to show that she fully understood God's command. Actually, God in the prohibition had not mentioned touching the tree. The word 'touching' involves more than a mere handling of the tree with the fingers. The word is pregnant in meaning, and apparently suggests touching in the sense of consuming or making the fruit one's own. Thus, for example, in Genesis 20:6 there is reference to Abimelech's touching Sarah, the wife of Abraham. Here, what is in view is not merely physical contact with another person, but the taking of that person sexually to be one's own. Again in Genesis 26:11 the word is used of the touching that would bring harm. Hence, we are safe in saying that Eve had more in mind than the mere feeling of the fruit with the fingers. She was not referring to handling of the fruit as such, but in all probability to that touching which would result in taking possession of the fruit and so consuming it.

At the same time she does not employ two precise synonyms. Even though to touch the fruit means to handle it so that one does in fact devour it, the emphasis in the verb is upon the act of touching itself. Hence, it would seem that Eve did truly understand God's command, and in the use of this word may have given expression to the truth that the outward act of partaking of the fruit was really the result or manifestation of an inward desire. If one would touch the fruit, that touching would lead to eating. It would not even be a true touching unless it resulted in a devouring of the fruit. It was the first step in the disobeying of God's command.

Lastly, the penalty which God had threatened is stated in general terms, and its forcefulness is weakened. Eve merely says, 'lest ye die,' whereas God had said, 'dying thou shalt die,' an idiom which means, 'thou shalt surely die.' Why did Eve do this? Why did she add to the commands of God? Why did she place them in her own words? Was she seeking by means of this exaggeration, if it be an exaggeration, to set a law for herself, as though to give to the serpent the impression that she was capable of stating what the law was? Possibly so, but it would seem that her exaggeration really revealed what was in her heart, namely, the feeling that God's prohibition had been too stringent. While not completely agreeing with the matter as phrased by the serpent, nevertheless, in her own heart, she was in agreement with him in thinking that God after all, had been too strict with her. It is a sad answer, for it reveals a heart all too willing and ready to listen to what the tempter had to say. It shows that Eve's love to God and her confidence and trust in Him had begun to waver. God was her creator, and to her and her husband He had been gracious. He had honoured her in creating her to be a help to the man, the crown of His creation. In developing the garden to God's glory she could be the man's help in a sense that was possible of none of the animals. But her confidence in her God was wavering; had He not after all, been too strict in His prohibition? This sad condition comes to the fore in the reply which she gives to the one whose only purpose was the destruction of her soul.

4. *And the serpent said unto the woman, Not dying shall ye die.*

Nowhere does Satan's unfairness and deceitfulness appear more clearly than here. Having first implanted a doubt in the woman's mind or at least having watered the doubt that may already have been there Satan now advances to a direct denial of God's truth. Having won the first round with Eve he is now in a position to deliver his knock-out blow. Hitherto the serpent had manifested what might be called a religious interest in the welfare of the woman. Now he changes his tactics. Now he is ready to engage in a direct denial of the truthfulness of what God has said. He gives to his lie all that he has, employing a forceful manner of expressing it. We may paraphrase, 'It is not true that ye shall surely die.' Careful students of the Bible have noted the nature of Satan's language. The negative comes first and receives all the emphasis, as though the evil one had thundered out, 'NO—it is not true that you will surely die.' It is a powerful negative, clearly spoken, so that Eve must now choose between God and the serpent. There can be no halfway station; either she must come out vigorously on the side of God or she must align herself with the serpent.

Satan shows himself to be an advocate of what today is often referred to as the 'new morality.' If there is anything that characterizes this 'new' morality it is that it is not new. In effect Satan is condemning the concept of absolute authority. The commands of God are harsh and stringent, he implies. They constrict the life so that they prohibit one from realizing life in all its potentialities and force him into a cramped narrow existence. Far more important than law, the tempter would seem to say, is love. He condemns Eve's attitude of trust in God's command and seeks to point out to her that if she would obtain the wholesomeness and well-roundedness that should characterize a fruitful life, she must not be bound by law.

Thus the serpent may proceed to his vicious task of impugning the motives of God. With sadness one reads his words, for the serpent is not fighting fairly. Yet so it is that Satan operates, and so it is that those who are on his side operate. Instead of death, he declares, Eve will receive knowledge, for God knows that in the day of her eating her eyes will be opened and she will be as God in that she will know good and evil.

The serpent makes it appear to Eve that he has a better knowledge of God than she has. She is confined by her position of trusting in God, of taking seriously His command that she will die if she disobeys. From this cramping position she must be emancipated and move over to a standpoint of 'neutrality' from which she can accurately pass judgment upon God and His commands. She is foolish to continue permitting God to lay down the law unto her.

Modern psychology, we can hear the tempter saying,

has brought to light the deep recesses of the human soul. That soul is a very tender thing, and to restrain and bind it by the imposition of categorical law is to harm it. The soul should be free to develop and to express itself, and this it can do only through freedom and love. Narrowness and restriction, such as absolute authority impose, must be abandoned, if there is to be any development of the personality. Would you be warped in your personality? If so, then continue submitting to God and His commandments. Those commandments may be sufficient for children, but not for one like yourself, Eve, who desires knowledge.

*5. For God knows that in the day that
ye eat thereof, ye shall be as God,
knowing good and evil.*

Tʜᴜs the serpent passes judgment
upon God. God is jealous, he suggests, and is imposing
His prohibition upon Adam and Eve lest they become
like Him, and then He will have rivals. What is said is
formally true, for actually when the man and the woman
do partake of the forbidden fruit their eyes are opened.
The truth however, is only formal. In a formal sense
their eyes would be opened, but the serpent does not
point out to Eve what the sad estate would be in which
they would have opened their eyes.

A minor question of interpretation confronts us here.
As is well known, the word for God in the Hebrew language is in the plural. Indeed, at this point, the King James
version has rendered, 'ye shall be as gods, knowing good
and evil.' If this be the correct interpretation then we are
to understand the serpent as saying that eating of the
forbidden tree will bring the woman and the man into
an equality with gods, or at least with divine beings.
Underlying this view is the assumption, it would seem,
that there actually are such beings, and should Adam and
Eve partake of the fruit of the tree of the knowledge

of good and evil, they could be like these beings.

In opposition to this, however, there are strong objections. Far better therefore, to render, 'ye shall become as God, knowing good and evil.' Satan is not concerned to tell the man and the woman that they will attain the plane of divine beings. His point is to oppose the God of goodness. He would make it appear to Adam and Eve that God in reality is not good, but jealous. If they eat, they will be like God, in that they will then know good and evil. Thus, in this light, it would appear that eating of the fruit is an act designed to spite God, and the words of the evil one have the purpose of painting a picture of God as jealous lest the man and woman become like Him.

Sometimes a half truth is more dangerous than an outright lie. God did know well enough that when the man and the woman disobeyed Him their eyes would be opened, and it was to prevent this sad consequence that He imposed His command. For God's commands are for our good. He does have a yoke, but that yoke is easy, and with Him there is a burden, but that burden is light. His law should be our delight, for it is good, and pure and holy. This the serpent denies. 'Not out of love and concern for your well being has God given this command,' he implies, 'but out of jealousy, lest ye become like Him. The fruit of the tree will not harm, as God's prohibition might seem to suggest.'

And thus the serpent holds out to them the prize of knowledge. To partake of this tree is the path to knowledge. To disobey the stringent prohibition of God and to assume the position of 'neutrality' from which one can properly estimate the words of God is the only thing to do if one would grow and develop in his personality. This is the path to knowledge. Abandon the blind attitude of faith and strike out on your own! Ahead of you lies knowledge, knowledge such as God Himself possesses. Here truly is a goal to strive after.

6. And the woman saw that the tree was good for food and that it was a desire to the eyes and to be desired was the tree to make one wise and she took from its fruit and she ate, and she gave also to her husband with her and he ate.

THE serpent does not in so many words urge the woman to partake of the forbidden fruit, nor is it necessary that he do so. In the false light that he casts upon it, the woman looks at the tree as though for the first time, and she sees just what the tempter desired her to see. Not the abomination of sin, not the hideousness of evil stand in her vision, for she has disavowed the faith, cast aside the word of God, accepted the lie, subjected herself to the devil, yielded to a mere sensual judgment, transgressed God's command and abandoned true knowledge in favour of the false.

Eve was no neutral, whether or not she realized the nature of her thoughts and actions. She did not look equally upon the commands of God and those of the evil one, for she was very definitely upon the side of the evil one, and her actions flowed from a heart that had fallen from God and was in bondage to sin. Eve followed what is sometimes called the 'scientific method.' She believed herself capable of evaluating all the facts of reality, including the fact of God and His commands, and passing upon them an impartial judgment. It was knowledge that she sought, and what higher aim could there be than that of comprehensive knowledge? She would know all things, and in the pursuit of that 'noble' aim she proceeded in a thoroughly careful manner. God had laid down certain commands, but these commands she must weigh in the light of the serpent's commentary. After all, it would be a foolish thing to claim that she knew the truth, to assert that because God had prohibited something, she should therefore obey. That would be tantamount to saying that the truth lay in what God had commanded, and that would be dogmatic indeed. Far better, far more thrilling would it be to engage in the pursuit of truth, to search for it wherever it might show itself. The commands of God had their place in the scheme of things, but Eve was a searcher after all truth, she desired to obtain comprehensive knowledge of the scheme of things, and hence, must consider seriously every suggestion that presented itself. Here was an avenue of fruitful research which she must not allow to remain uninvestigated. After all, the serpent's words were worthy of consideration; he might be right after all. Surely she should listen to him and pay heed to what he had to say! After all, he was only trying to help her.

And what was this knowledge that the serpent offered to her? The tree of the knowledge of good and evil! Those words were interesting; good and evil, what did they mean? At this point a knowledge of the languages of the ancient world may be of some aid in our understanding of Genesis. In the ancient Egyptian language, for example, the phrase 'good and evil' was a synonym for the expression 'everything.' Hence, to say that a man knew good and evil meant that he knew everything.

Here, however, the words are not merely a synonym for the word 'everything' for their content is far richer. Yet it is the goal of comprehensive knowledge that the tempter does place before Eve but this knowledge is conceived as consisting both of good and evil. In the phrase the good and evil are set side by side as opposing concepts. Good stands in opposition to evil and evil to good. Had man continued as he was, not giving heed to the serpent, he would have known to distinguish the good from the evil, to choose the one and to reject the other.

To Eve however, the temptation is offered to disobey God so that she will know good and evil. The word 'know' is pregnant in meaning, signifying more than a mere intellectual understanding. It involves an experiencing, so that for Eve to know good and evil as the serpent suggested would be an experiencing of good and evil. It would however, have been an experiencing from the standpoint of one who had fallen into sin. Eve could look back to that time when she was good and delighted in obedience to God and contrast it with the present when she found her delight in the doing of evil. From the standpoint of a fallen creature Eve would know the difference between good and evil, should she hearken to the serpent's voice.

Perhaps it would be well to note that the serpent actually does hold out to Eve this goal of knowledge. Some would interpret his words to read, 'Ye shall be as God who knows good and evil.' This is a possible rendering of the Hebrew, but it involves a difficulty, for it does not really tell Eve in what respect she will be like God. It would seem to be better therefore to translate the words as is ordinarily done, 'Ye shall be as God, in that ye shall be knowers of good and evil.'

What a sharp contrast this was from what God intended for the man and woman! 'Do the evil,' the tempter was saying in effect, 'in order that you may know the difference between good and evil, from the point of view of evil.' How different was God's desire that they, merely out of love for Him and obedience to His command, simply because it was His command, should know the difference between good and evil! That God's law should be the delight of the heart leads to an obedience of God's commands born out of love to God. When the Saviour came to earth He said, 'I delight to do thy will.' Had Adam and Eve out of mere love of God obeyed His commands, they would truly have been blessed. Far better it is to say, 'God commands this, and although I may not understand all the implications of His command nor even see the reason why He has uttered it, nevertheless, because I love Him, my delight is to obey Him. Merely because He commands is a far stronger reason than all the reason that the evil one can amass to entice me to disobey Him.' Thus the heart of trust and faith would speak. Whatever reasons Satan may produce, they do not equal in compelling power the fact that God has spoken. God's mere command is sufficient reason for obedience.

To Satan, however, the life of faith and simple trust in God is abhorrent. There can be nothing more unscientific; nothing more obscurantist in his eyes. But Satan did not understand the truth of God's command, nor did the reason for it impress him in the least. Actually his words to Eve imply that there is a magical quality in the fruit. 'If you partake of this fruit,' he says in effect, 'you will not die. On the other hand, to partake of this fruit is to bring to you the knowledge of good and evil, and that is a knowledge which you do not now have.' Here then is the first of that long series of misinterpretations which would see in the fruit of the tree itself something harmful or evil. And this is to sink to the level of magic. The high, pure ground of the spiritual which had underlain God's good prohibition is thrown aside, and the cheap, low level of magic is substituted. Thus the tempter debases the argument. He cannot understand that one might so love God that the mere love of God would be sufficient for him, so that whatever God might command, he would obey, simply because the One he loved had commanded it Not so Satan, for he is the god of confusion and superstition. Hence, in his language he blurs the truth so that the situation will appear confused to Eve, and she will look upon the fruit as though in itself it had the power to bestow upon her the coveted gift of knowledge.

And Eve was deceived. She saw as she had not seen before. It is quite possible that the phrase 'and the woman saw,' means 'and the woman gave heed to.' Thus, in Genesis 30:1 we read, 'And Rachel saw that she had not borne to Jacob.' (Cf. also verse 9.) What is meant is that Rachel realized or gave heed to the fact that she had not yet borne sons to Jacob. Likewise in the passage before us, Eve now turned her attention to the tree as she had not done previously. She had seen the tree before, but she had never looked at the fruit with that intensity and consideration that now filled her gaze. She looked upon this fruit, for she thought that it had the power to give her something that she did not possess.

Prominent in Eve's glance is the sensual and material. It is the tree which is good for food, for if she ate of this tree it would raise her to the place of God. Like the serpent she too now apparently regards the tree as possessing magical qualities. God had planted the garden with trees that were good for food and pleasant to the sight (Genesis 2:9), but Eve now believes, for she has listened to the evil one, that this particular tree, more than any of the others, is good for food, for the food of this particular tree will bestow upon her a coveted object, the knowledge of good and evil.

In addition the tree was a delight to the eyes. From the coarsely sensual aspect she turns to the more aesthetic. Yet in a special sense this tree is a delight to the eyes. In His goodness God had placed the man and woman in a garden in which all the trees were a delight to the sight, but now this one tree stands out in Eve's eyes. Perhaps it is with intention that Moses here uses the word 'eyes,' for it was through partaking of the fruit of this tree that the eyes of both the man and his wife were opened. The tree was also to be desired to make one wise, for it brought discernment between good and evil, the knowledge that Eve so coveted. What greater enticement than this can there be?

Coupled with the woman's reflection upon the tree there was doubtless the use of her imagination, and in this imagination she greatly magnified the effects that would accrue from partaking of the forbidden fruit. How powerfully this all weighed with her as over against the simple command of God! First reflection appears in her heart, then lust or desire and then the overt action. Here is exemplified the truth that as a man thinketh in his heart, so is he. To reflect upon the desirability of sin is to take the first step toward that outward act that the Scripture condemns.

And so it was with Eve. The matter was in her heart, but it did not stay there. Her perception and the flight of her imagination were followed immediately by decision and action. In simple direct language the Bible states, 'and she took from its fruit, and she ate.' In all their stark aloneness, the words stand out. Moses adds no comment; he expresses no shock, he makes no observations. The mere words recording the tragic action are sufficient. Eve's love of God and her trust in Him were not strong enough; she was unwilling to obey Him merely because He had commanded. The bare statement is in itself sufficient. Eve disobeyed God; she permitted herself to be deceived by the arch-deceiver.

Not only did she herself partake but she also gave of the fruit to her husband who was with her, and he did eat. We are not told what kind of fruit it was, nor is there need to know. The old tradition that the fruit was an apple rests upon a confusion of the Latin word *malum* (apple) with the Latin word *malus* (evil). In the genitive case the two words would have had the same form, namely, *mali*. Nor is it important that we know what kind of fruit it was; Eve led her husband into sin, for he too ate. Even in sin he is not alone. For his highest development the man needed a help, but the help has become a hindrance. She is the occasion of his disobedience, and in the transgression she is with him. Her first act is to give him of the fruit.

Adam is said to have been 'with her,' an expression which quite possibly may mean that he was not merely there present but that he was also associating himself with Eve in her act. Up until this point no word has been uttered concerning Adam. Where he had been we do not know. Had he been present listening to the entire conversation between the serpent and the woman?—one cannot say. All that we do know is that at the moment when Eve actually partook of the fruit Adam was present, and apparently had done nothing to dissuade her from her action. 'And he ate.' With those words the verse comes to a close. Thus, the command of God is trampled underfoot. He who had done so much for the man, placing him as the lord of creation in the garden of beauty, is now rejected. The all-wise, all-knowing God had said, 'Thou shalt surely die.' The creature, however, did not love God; 'and he ate.'

Simple and direct as is the language of the Bible, it nevertheless raises a number of problems. For one thing, how could Adam have eaten the forbidden fruit? God had created Adam holy and free from sin. Indeed, we read, 'And God saw everything that he had made, and behold it was very good!' (Genesis 1:31). This includes Adam also. Upon the created man God could pronounce the judgment, 'Very good.' How then could a creature that was very good do that which was evil? The man was not compelled from without to make a choice of evil. He was truly a responsible, free being, who acted because he wished to. He himself, his nature, disposition and character, determine what he will do, and in accordance with that nature, disposition and character he acts. He cannot, however, act or make choices which are contrary to his nature, disposition and character. God, for example, who is good, cannot act contrary to His nature He cannot lie. Sinful acts proceed from a sinful nature. In sinning, Adam showed that he possessed a sinful nature. Inasmuch as he was created good, however, whence came this sinful nature? We cannot understand, for God has not revealed how a disposition that is holy can change to one that is unholy. How, in other words, could sin find an entrance into a soul that was created holy? Adam and Eve were created with pure moral character, upright and holy in their nature. Yet, their nature changed, and from this changed nature sinful acts flowed forth. To us the problem is insoluble and yet, if we are to do justice to the Scripture, its existence must be acknowledged. How could sin find lodgement in a holy soul? Although we are not able to give a satisfactory answer to this question, nevertheless, the fact is that the nature of our first parents did change. Although created holy, they notwithstanding acted as holy creatures cannot act; they sinned against God, and thus by sinning revealed that their action proceeded from a depraved and corrupt nature.

When, however, did this change in the nature of our first parents occur? The answer to this question is also difficult. It has been held that the mysterious change and the overt transgression are bound up together, so that we cannot necessarily say that the change took place temporally before the act of transgression. It has also been held that when Eve looked at the tree, thus influenced by the subtle suggestion of Satan, the change had already taken place. It is also possible that when Satan first approached her, the change had occurred. It does seem strange that she saw nothing out of place in an animal acting as a man, indeed setting itself above man and on an equality with God.

In the light of the superior position which had been assigned to man in 2:19 it is strange that Eve did not react to the approach of the serpent in an unfavourable manner. It is also strange that in her language to the serpent she misrepresented the prohibition of God. On the basis of these two considerations there are those who think that the tragic change in nature may have occurred when the tempter approached and that this change manifested itself almost immediately in Eve's partaking of the forbidden fruit. One thing is surely clear. When she actually partook of the forbidden fruit, Eve acted as an enemy of God. As created, however, she was neither mortal nor sinful.

'In Adam's fall, we sinned all.'

Thus stand the words in the New England primer. But did Adam fall? Genesis says, 'and he ate,' but did he eat? Those are the questions that now confront us, and we cannot go on with a study of the chapter until we have settled them. In what we have thus far written we have assumed that the text of Genesis relates something that actually took place. Eve was in the garden; she was tempted of the evil one; she did eat and she gave to her husband with her and he ate also. Have we, however, been justified in interpreting Genesis in this way? May we not completely have misunderstood the intention of Genesis? Instead of understanding it as relating something historical, may not its purpose be quite different? Is it not conceivable that in regarding Adam as an historical character we have completely missed the point of Genesis?.

There are those who tell us that such is the case. In regarding Adam as a man who once lived upon this earth, they say, we have exhibited a naïveté that ill becomes those who would seriously understand the Bible. In insisting upon an historical interpretation of the first book of Scripture we have obscured and overlooked the deep and profound teaching which is really found therein. Such a charge cannot lightly be brushed aside. Surely no Christian would want to misinterpret God's holy and infallible Word, and to do so would be particularly unfortunate with respect to the important and significant early chapters of Genesis.

May not these early chapters be regarded as parables? A parable is a story which may or may not be true; it may or may not have taken place. The important thing is that a parable conveys a meaning and that meaning is more important than whether the parable tells of a happening that did actually take place. In Nathan's parable to David, for example, our main concern is with the cruelty of the rich man who stole the ewe lamb from the poor man and gave it to the traveller. This is of far greater import than whether the story ever actually took place. That we may abhor such an act of cruelty and violence is the lesson which the parable should inculcate, and if we spend too much time considering whether the story is true or not we may lose its message. That would be a tragedy indeed! What is of significance then, is not the actual language of the parable, but the meaning that lies beyond it, a meaning that is spiritual in nature.

If then the third chapter of Genesis is a parable, we should read it as a parable, considering it as poetry rather than as prose narrative, remembering that it makes use of poetic imagery and symbols. To treat these as though we were reading ordinary historical prose is simply to mistake the nature of Genesis three. Here, in this chapter such images abound, the serpent, the tree of life, the tree of the knowledge of good and evil, the garden, the fruit, the sword, the cherubim. To conceive of the man and woman as actual living human beings who lived in a garden, we are told, is to mistake the meaning of the chapter. Adam was not a real, individual man, nor Eve a real individual woman, nor was Eden a garden that could be located geographically. Rather, all these things are poetic figures that belong to the realm of poetic imagery and symbolism and not to history and geography, and the kind of truth with which they have to do is not of the same order as that of history and science. This truth of the poetic symbols is ultimate truth which can be grasped only by the imagination, not as a result of historical study and investigation. It cannot be revealed in ordinary simple statements but only through symbol and image. This ultimate truth is personal, and so it is held that Genesis three does not teach us about the fall of the first man into sin, as at first sight it might seem to do, but rather it teaches me as an individual that I am alienated from God and need to be reconciled to Him. And then, all too often it is said today, 'I am Adam,' or, as some would put it, 'Every man is Adam.' Only when as an individual I understand this 'existential truth' that I am Adam and that the words of Genesis are addressed to me, can I begin to understand the chapter and the general truths which may also be contained therein.

It is sometimes said that this ultimate truth is really the truth of religious awareness, and that this truth cannot be communicated to us by means of intellectual propositions, but must be expressed in image and symbol. The propositions, such as 'Christ died for sinners,' are not the actual revelation, so we are told, but are merely the inference from the revelation which God gives to us through images, symbols and persons. The actual revelation occurs when I am confronted with the truth that I am a fallen creature in need of God's salvation. Through the words of the Scripture I have an encounter with God and that is the revelation as a present reality.

All of this is very interesting. It has been set forth in a number of ways by many modern writers who are sincere students of the Bible, but who, we believe, are sincerely in error. Is the purpose of Genesis three to teach me that I am Adam and that only when, in reading the words of this chapter, I am confronted with that truth and can realize that I am alienated from God by my sin? Certainly it would be difficult to derive such a meaning from the chapter itself.

And this is the first point that we wish to make. A simple reading of the Bible would not lead one to the position that ultimate truth can only be expressed in image and symbol and that the individual reader is Adam. The position which we have just set forth briefly is not taught in the Bible nor can it be derived from a simple reading of Scripture. It comes from elsewhere. It is imposed upon the Bible from without; it is not Biblical. That in itself should be sufficient to condemn it. This interpretation has its roots not in the Bible but in the writings of certain philosophers. In its essence it is irrational and not Biblical.

We must also take note that this modern interpretation of Genesis three actually makes claims that cannot be substantiated. To say that propositional statements are merely inferences of the truth and not expressions of the truth itself is contrary to Scripture. When the Bible tells us that God is love, is that merely an inference or is that the truth? Were it not for the revelation of the Bible, expressed in the words, 'God is love,' we would not know that such was the case. We have learned that God is love, simply because the Bible tells us so. Our knowledge of that truth may have been confirmed through images and symbols, but the actual truth itself is conveyed to us in those simple words.

Did Jesus Christ die to save sinners or did He not? When we say that He did are we merely drawing an inference from a truth that has been given to us through image or symbol? Obviously we are not. The Scripture states plainly that Christ died to save sinners, and that is how we know that He died. Were it not for the plain words of the Bible, we would not know that the death of our Lord saved us from our sins. The actual words, the propositional statements, are what tell us that we are saved.

If we are to depend upon a revelation through persons and symbols without an accompanying explanation in words we are of all men most miserable.

Let us not be ashamed to acknowledge that God in His goodness has spoken to mankind. He has given to us His Word, and that Word is filled with propositions which express the truth. Thus, His very Word is the truth and not a mere inference drawn from the truth. God is love; God created the heaven and the earth; Christ died for my sin; Christ rose from the dead; this same Jesus will so come again. All of these are propositional statements which teach the truth. They are the revelation from God. To assert that ultimate truth cannot be communicated to man in propositional statements is to talk utter nonsense. God has revealed such truth, and the whole Bible is His revelation. We are to interpret that revelation in the sense intended by its individual parts, but the entirety of the Bible is the revelation of God.

In this grand revelation there is a remarkable variety, to be sure. Prose and poetry are found there, an abundance of symbols and figures of speech. We are to interpret them as their sense demands. When we read prose, we are so to interpret it. Likewise with poetry. Figures of speech and symbols we are to recognize as such. One thing, however, we are not to do. We are not to interpret prose as though it were poetry. We are not to consider historical characters as though they were mere symbols. To deny the historicity of Genesis three is a serious thing, but the man who says, 'The writer of Genesis three believed that Adam was an historical character, but I do not agree with him,' is a far better interpreter of the

Bible than the one who declares that although Adam was not an historical character, Genesis three is nevertheless profoundly true. For if Adam was not an historical person, then the study of Genesis three is little more than a waste of time.

Should we read Genesis three as poetry and not as prose? For our part we can see no reason for so doing, and we wonder if it would be asking too much of those who make this assertion that they provide just a bit of evidence to support their position. We confess to becoming a little tired of reading dogmatic assertions about how Genesis three is to be interpreted when these assertions are accompanied by no evidence. The mere declaration that we misunderstand the chapter if we think that Adam was a real person who lived in a garden is not sufficient argument to lead us to agree. And the constantly reiterated error that ultimate truth cannot be given to man in propositional statements should, at least occasionally, be supported by evidence.

On the other hand, there is sufficient evidence to show us that we should read the third chapter of the Bible as prose and not as poetry. For one thing the characteristics of Hebrew poetry are missing in this chapter. If the writer, whom we believe to be Moses, wanted to write poetry, why did he not do so? Why did he make his writing look so much like prose that men thus naturally interpret it? Hebrew poetry is characterized by parallelism, in which two lines or parts of lines bear a parallel relationship one to another. Such parallelism is lacking for the most part in chapter three.

Furthermore a parable is told in order to inculcate a

lesson or to become the basis for a message. After Nathan had told his parable to David he proceeded to preach to the king. In the parables of our Lord we find a didactic purpose. He uses them in order to present a message. Nothing like that occurs here. No lesson is drawn from Adam's and Eve's action; no sermon is preached; no message is given. If this third chapter of Genesis is a parable, it would have been a help if the writer had given some indication of the fact.

Everything in the chapter leads to the conclusion that the writer is giving straightforward prose. He believes that he is writing about certain things that did actually take place. This is shown for one thing in the manner in which chapter two prepares for the events of chapter three. The third chapter does not stand as an isolated unit. Indeed, divorce it from what precedes and from what follows and it does not yield a good sense. For its proper understanding we are dependent both upon what goes before and upon what comes after.

The man and the woman are the same in both chapters two and three. Chapter two tells of the creation of the man and of the relationship in which the woman stands to him. Emphasis falls upon the garden which God had prepared for them. Were Moses writing a mere parable, intended to teach a lesson, it is surprising that he should give so much time to detail. As one reads of the rivers of the garden, it is as though the writer is going out of his way to fix the garden's location, so that there will be no mistaking that location. If this is a parable, such detailed description is strange indeed. Read the various parables in the Bible, both in the Old and in the New Testament, and the one thing that stands out is the absence of detail in the telling of the parable. All the stress falls, not upon detail, but upon the lesson which the parable is to teach. Our Lord's parables were brief, and pointed, but that is not the case with Genesis. Our Lord's parables led to a message: Genesis puts stress upon detail and leads to no message as do parables. If Genesis three is a parable, it is a parable without equal.

Another consideration also shows that we are not dealing with a parable. The history of Adam and Eve continues in what follows, and the sad condition of the world is shown to be the result of what Adam and Eve did. Moses' purpose seems to be to indicate that the condition of the world is due to the act of Adam. If this is his purpose, it is clear that he is purporting to write an account of what actually took place and not a parable. Indeed, if Genesis three is a parable, we are left without any real explanation of how the world came into the sinful condition in which it appears in Genesis four. All of this makes it clear that the writer at least thought he was writing an explanation of the entrance of sin into the world.

What settles the question once and for all is the witness of the New Testament. 'Wherefore,' writes the apostle Paul in Romans 5:12, 'as by one man sin entered into the world, and death by sin . . .'. This is a clear-cut and explicit assertion that sin entered into the world by one man. Again, in 2 Corinthians 11:3, 'But I fear, lest by any means, as the serpent beguiled Eve through his subtilty, so your minds should be corrupted from the simplicity that is in Christ.' There is no mistaking the manner in which Paul refers to the serpent beguiling Eve. If Eve is simply a symbol, there would not be much point in Paul speaking as he did. 'For Adam was first formed, then Eve. And Adam was not deceived, but the woman being deceived was in the transgression' (1 Timothy 2:13, 14). Unless Adam and Eve were historical characters, Paul's argument loses its force.

Inasmuch as the New Testament is the Word of God, whatever it asserts is the truth, and when the New Testament speaks of Adam and Eve as historical, the question is settled. But is it not dishonest thus to appeal to the New Testament? There are those who assert that it is. We must study the Old Testament upon its merits, so they tell us; we cannot take refuge in appeals to the New Testament; to do so is to engage in dishonest scholarship.

Of course the first task of the earnest and conscientious student of Scripture must be to ascertain the meaning of the passage which he is studying. This is not always easy, but it is a task which should not be shirked. At the same time, the Old Testament is a preparation for the New, and the proper interpretation of the Old Testament is found in the New. If, then, one disregards the New Testament he will never properly explain the Old. The prophecies, for example, can to a certain extent be understood from the Old Testament, but they can never be grasped in their fulness as they should be, unless we take into consideration the further revelation which God has given to us in the New Testament. In order to do justice to any verse of Scripture we must take into account all that the Bible has to say upon it. Neglect of this principle simply leads to false interpretation. No serious student of the Bible who conscientiously considers all that the Bible has to say about the events recorded in Genesis three could come to the conclusion that the chapter was a parable. And to neglect what the New Testament teaches is not to do justice to Genesis three. We make no apology for referring to the further revelation of the New Testament; indeed, only by so doing can we properly understand the chapter which we are now studying. And the New Testament makes it clear that the events of Genesis three are historical. There was an Adam and there was an Eve; there was a garden and a serpent. We are not dealing with a parable, but with an account of those sad events which once occurred in the historical garden of Eden. The New Testament has spoken; with its infallible declarations we can rest content.

Biblical parables are clear as to their meaning. One thing that characterizes them is their perspicuity. When we read the parable of the ewe lamb we know what its lesson is. What it is teaching is not something dark and obscure, but something clear. What, however, is the lesson that Genesis three is supposed to teach, if it be a parable? If it is intended to teach that each one of us who reads it is Adam, then its teaching is not clear. For years, throughout the history of the Christian church, no one seems to have understood the parable. And this is strange. Some of the best minds of the church such as Augustine, Calvin and Luther have written expositions of the passage, and none of them seems to have caught the lesson that they themselves were Adam. Indeed, even the New Testament seems to have slipped up here. Paul should have seen that he himself was Adam; instead of that he missed the point completely and regarded Adam as an historical character. And if this stricture be applied to Augustine, Calvin, Luther and even Paul, we must go a step further and note that even our Lord Jesus Christ failed to understand the meaning of the 'parable' of Genesis three. For He spoke of the devil as being a murderer from the beginning who did not stand in the truth (John 8:44). The close connection between the lie and murder in Christ's words shows that they reflect upon the events recorded in Genesis three. In Matthew 13:38 He speaks of the tares as being the sons of the evil one, and in the thirty-ninth verse declares that the enemy who has sown these tares is the devil. Here there seems to be reflection on the language of Genesis 3:15. It is surely clear that the Lord of glory thought that the events of Genesis three were historical events. Not a word that fell from His holy lips lends strength to the view that the third chapter of Genesis is merely a parable.

If we conceive of Adam as a real, individual man or of Eden as a garden that actually existed and could be located geographically we sadly misconceive the symbolism of Genesis! That is a serious charge indeed. Luther seriously misconceived this symbolism, so did Calvin and Augustine, so did Paul, and most important of all, so did the Lord Jesus Christ, the omniscient Son of God. In fact the only ones who have not thus seriously misconceived of this 'symbolism' are the scholars of today who do not regard the Bible as the infallible and inerrant revelation of the one living and true God. That Christ and the apostles interpreted Genesis three as an historical document should be sufficient for the humble Christian who desires to follow in their steps.

It remains to note that the lesson that I am Adam is a lesson that does not make much sense. Adam, we are often told, is everyman, and his experience that of everyman. When I realize that I am Adam and that I have transgressed and am estranged, so runs the argument, then I understand the chapter and have appreciated its lesson. But is not this so-called lesson of Genesis three rather a far-fetched and silly kind of thing? Say what one will, my experience is not that of Adam, nor for that matter, is the experience of anyone else. Adam went through a unique experience. What happened to him does not happen to me nor to anyone else, and to declare that I am Adam and that my experience is his is to talk nonsense.

When Adam sinned, he fell from an estate of being good into an estate of being evil. He was created by God as a creature of whom it could be said that he was 'very good.' From this estate in which he was created by God he fell into an estate of sin and misery and by his disobedience plunged all men into that same estate of sin and misery. That is not true of me. My sin has not plunged all men into an estate of sin and misery. Furthermore, by my sin I did not fall from an estate of being 'very good' into an estate of evil. I and all men like me were born into that miserable estate of sin, and when we sinned we simply showed that we were in such an estate. By sinning Adam became a sinner; by sinning we do not become sinners, we are already sinners. Sin does not cause us to fall from the estate wherein we were created, for we were born into a fallen estate. With Adam, however, the case was quite different. His sin brought him into a fallen estate. By disobedience he fell; by disobedience we simply show that we are already fallen. Hence, the experience of Adam was unique; it is his experience alone and not that of myself or of everyman.

Perhaps we should note again the stress that Paul places upon the historicity of Adam. It would be well to read Romans 5:12ff. carefully. In these verses Paul constantly reasons as though there had been a real man named Adam and attributes to the disobedience of this man the fallen condition of the remainder of mankind. His phrases are cogent: as by one man sin entered into the world—the similitude of Adam's transgression—the offence of one—one that sinned—the judgment was by one to condemnation—by one man's offence death reigned by one—by the offence of one . . . upon all men unto condemnation—one man's disobedience.

In these words of the apostle the uniqueness of Adam stands out. No other man is thus contrasted with Christ. It is the work of Adam as over against that of Christ. Indeed, elsewhere Paul speaks of Christ as the second Adam. Suppose, however, that Paul is mistaken! Suppose that Adam was not a real individual and had never lived! What becomes of the point of Paul's tremendous argument? It then loses all its force. All that Paul says about the saving work of Christ is lost if there was no first Adam to bring the world into sin. Indeed, it follows that if Adam is not an historical character, what Paul writes concerning Christ must be rejected. If Adam is unreal, the contrast which Paul makes is false, and Paul's statements concerning the work of Christ must be rejected. None of them are then true. If there was no first Adam, then Christ is not the second Adam. And this leads us to the heart of the matter. If Paul was so profoundly mistaken about Adam, how do we know that he was not equally mistaken about Christ? If Adam is not an historical character, how do we know that Christ was an historical character? And further, if we do not need to believe that Adam was a real individual, why do we have to believe that Christ was a real individual? Remove Adam and his historicity from these verses and all the profound truths that Paul is teaching go by the board. They are then not truths at all and Paul's words must be abandoned. Adam is gone, but so is Christ. Let him who will be content with the shadowy view that Adam is everyone. His view may fit in with certain modern philosophical positions, but it is not the teaching of the Holy Word of God. The terrible act that brought about our death is stated in the simple words, 'and he did eat,' and these words are true.

This brings us to the consideration of a strange fact. Of all the documents that have come down from antiquity, Genesis three is the only one that explains how the world became sinful and evil. At first sight it might seem that this statement could be challenged, but if we examine carefully the legacy which the near eastern world has left, we discover that it is true. In some of these documents a contrast is indeed presented between a time when all seems to have been well and one when all was not well. What produced the change, however? It is this question which is really unanswered. Furthermore, at best what the ancient documents give us is a contrast between a period of bliss and one when things are out of joint. They do not seriously consider the question of moral evil; they do not picture man as estranged from a holy God. To suggest that the author of Genesis three was influenced by these writings is to betray an ignorance of the facts. Genesis three is unique; its like is not to be found in the ancient world. And the reason for this is not far to seek. The third chapter of the Bible is the word of the one true God who created man; the writings of the ancient near east are the work of men whose minds were steeped in ignorance and the darkness of superstition.

Before we proceed with the interpretation of our chapter we must examine more closely than hitherto precisely what was the nature of the temptation and precisely what it was that the tempter held out to Eve. What actually happened when Adam and his wife partook of the forbidden fruit?

The tree in the midst of the garden is designated the tree of the knowledge of good and evil. Some have suggested that this designation means the tree of the knowledge of good and the tree of the knowledge of evil. It was thus, on this interpretation a tree whose knowledge might be that of good or of evil. Had man sustained his probation he might have eaten of the tree and received the knowledge of good. Should he disobey it would be a tree of the knowledge of evil. This can hardly be the meaning of the phrase, for after the fall, man is said to know good and evil. Furthermore, the phrase does not really permit of a breaking up in this way. Rather, as we have earlier sought to point out it is good and evil in contrast which are designated by the phrase. Good and evil mutually condition one another and form a complex.

In what respect, however, would man attain unto this knowledge? There is one opinion which from time to time keeps raising its head, and which must be briefly considered. In a fairly recent form the view is as follows: The tree is said to be supernatural, and the knowledge which would accrue to man from eating thereof was such as belonged to God alone and which would be fatal for man. Yet when man ate of the tree, death did not come to him, but rather the realization that he was naked. Thus there came to Adam and Eve the consciousness of sex. To have such knowledge would make man like God, for man could now reproduce and produce life. In this sense he was like God, for as God could create, so also now could man, by creating new beings like himself. Why, however, should such knowledge be thought to be death bringing? Strange indeed is the answer that is given. Inasmuch as the production of life in time will fill the earth, death must come in order that the world be not over-populated. As the inevitable consequence of Adam's ability to increase the race, death comes.

With this interpretation of the Scripture we cannot for a moment agree. For one thing it regards the chapter merely as a legend; it denies the historicity of Adam, and for that reason alone, if for no other, should be decisively rejected. It is not correct to say that Adam did not die when he ate the forbidden fruit. Adam immediately fell into an estate of sin and misery and this estate was one which brought him to death. He did die, although not in a physical sense, the moment he disobeyed God.

Nor is it correct to say that the consciousness of sex came to man upon eating of the forbidden fruit. In the

first chapter of Genesis man was commanded to be fruitful and to fill the earth. Before the entrance of sin into
the world, man knew about sex. He knew that it was good
and noble and that he might use it for God's glory and
for the fulfilment of God's command. With the entrance
of sin into the world, however, man's evaluation of sex
changed. From now on he interpreted sex, as he interpreted everything else, from a wrong standpoint. Hence,
man now looks upon nakedness as something of which
to be ashamed.

Death then came upon man not because there was
danger that in producing life he would over-populate
the world, but simply because he had disobeyed God.

7. *And there were opened the eyes of the two of them and they knew that naked were they, and they sewed the leaf of the fig tree and they made for themselves girdles*

*H*AD the serpent spoken the truth? Scripture says that their eyes were opened, and that is precisely what the tempter had predicted. But to what were their eyes opened? Did Adam and Eve now possess that desired knowledge which the serpent had promised would be theirs if they disobeyed? An unexpected development occurs, something that Adam and Eve had not looked for. From the formal standpoint the words of the serpent were true, but these 'true' words of the tempter expressed a tremendous lie. And this fact should be a warning. It is possible to say something that in itself is true and by so doing to give an entirely erroneous impression. This is deceitfulness, and to do this deliberately is to sin grievously. Our speech must be filled with caution, lest even unintentionally our words give to men a false impression. Our great responsibility is as far as we are able to convey only the truth when we speak. Better not to speak at all than by careless words, even when they are formally correct, to convey an impression that is contrary to fact.

Satan's action, however, was not careless, but deliberate. No friend of man was he, but the arch-deceiver. Apart from the lie he cannot carry on his work. How great a mistake we make if we assume that Satan in his opposition to God fights out in the open! His lies are not open and direct, for the art of deceitfulness serves him far better. No match for Satan are we, if we fight him in our own strength. He can and will far outsmart us, for he goes about as a roaring lion seeking whom he may devour. There is One however, who has vanquished Satan, and in His strength, and alone in His strength, we can conquer. He has conquered the evil one, and He has done so by means that are just and true. Of His battle we need never be ashamed.

Now Adam and Eve see good and evil from the stand-point of sinners, from the low level of sin. Their eyes were opened to the fact that they were corrupt and polluted, for they sought both to clothe themselves and to hide from the presence of God. To all the miseries that this life brings their eyes are opened, and they now begin to see things which formerly they had not noticed. They see now that they were naked, and they furthermore regarded this nakedness as a cause for shame. The knowledge which the serpent had promised, that of good and evil, proved to be a knowledge that would destroy them.

It is not of the physical eyes that the Scripture speaks here, when it states that 'their eyes were opened,' for Adam and Eve had not been physically blind, nor had their physical eyes formerly been closed so that they could not see. Rather, the reference is to the arousing of the conscience and an awakening of the understanding so that the man and the woman now see themselves in a tragic condition and seek deliverance therefrom. They recognize their lost condition and realize from what a high estate they have fallen. They see evil in distinction from good as before they had not done.

At this point Scripture does not explicitly respond to the prohibition of Genesis 2:17 with the statement that Adam and Eve died. Nevertheless, in the declaration that their eyes were opened, the same truth is really taught. The words 'ye shall surely die' would seem to have a primary reference to physical death, for it is physical death which cuts man off from life upon this earth and which shows that man is not to live eternally upon the earth. At the same time the narrative makes clear that Adam and Eve were now in a condition in which they possessed a corruption of heart (as shown both by their endeavour to clothe their nakedness, and also by their shame) and that in addition they were guilty before God (as seen in their attempt to hide themselves from Him). Finally they were banished from His presence, and herein is the essence of death, namely, separation from God. As surely as they ate from the forbidden fruit, therefore, so surely did the man and his wife fall into an estate in which the seed of death was in their heart, a seed which would ripen and break forth in actual physical death, and which would separate them from their Maker and so lead them ultimately to complete separation from God.

A certain emphasis in the chapter falls upon the words 'know' and 'knowledge.' There is the tree of the knowledge of good and evil; and according to the serpent, 'God knows' what will eventuate from eating the forbidden fruit. Now again, we read, 'and they knew.' Once more it appears that in a formal sense the words of the serpent were true. Knowledge would indeed result from partaking of the forbidden fruit, yet what knowledge it was! In place of a wonderful knowledge such as the tempter's words might have led them to expect, they find that they are naked; the promised richness has become poverty and misery. What a knowledge this was! They now know that they are naked, and nakedness produces shame.

Before the fall the first man and woman saw things as they actually were. Wherever they cast their eyes they beheld the world that their good God had created and they saw all things as His creation. To Him they raised their hearts in adoration and praise, for He had granted to them a full and rich world in which to live. Thus beholding the world and all things as coming from the hand of God, they had seen their nakedness as something which came from Him and as something which produced no shame in their hearts.

The knowledge which they now have is one which judges everything from a false standpoint. It sees all from a perverted position. Basically it is mistaken about all that it would interpret. And so nakedness becomes a matter of shame. As unfallen creatures the man and his wife had rejoiced in all things. Now, because of sin, they can really rejoice in nothing.

As a result they seek to do what sinners always try to do. They make an effort at saving themselves. So perverted is their reason, so dark their light, so ignorant their knowledge, that they fall into the foolish effort of attempting to clothe their nakedness. It is the first attempt at salvation by works, and it is just as ineffectual as all such attempts. Man cannot do the impossible, and it is impossible that a fallen creature by his own efforts should clothe his nakedness and present himself before God. The action is an admission that all is not well; a confession that the heart is polluted.

In the garden before the fall the man and woman acted in accordance with God's command. His will was their law, and they gladly yielded thereto a rejoicing obedience. Now that they have fallen and become estranged from God, however, they act upon their own. Without asking God, they proceed right away to sew for themselves girdles in order thereby to provide clothing.

From God they would hide themselves and also from one another. Nor is it merely their nakedness that they would hide. Actually in every aspect of life they must hide something from each other. Sin is secretive and breaks a pure and open fellowship. The blessed communion and companionship of Paradise is shattered, for sin is essentially divisive.

We have no warrant for assuming that the tree of the knowledge of good and evil was a fig tree and that for that reason they used the leaf of a fig tree in sewing their girdles. Rather, it would seem that they used the fig tree because of the size of the leaf and its suitableness for the purpose. Nor need we be too disturbed to learn that the fig tree is not common to Babylonia. Apparently it does grow in mountain ranges of the south Iranian plateau and in Kurdistan and Asia Minor.

Several rather exotic interpretations of the fig tree have been introduced by commentators. According to some the use of the girdles indicated the beginning of cultivated civilization. But this narrative of Scripture is not talking about culture. Such a thought is simply read into the text; it is not found there. Others assert that the tree had a magical power to work an aphrodisiac effect. This of course is not what the Scripture means. Perhaps it will not be out of place to repeat that the tree had no magical effects. Not through magic did death enter the world but simply through disobedience to God.

8. And they heard the voice of the Lord God walking in the garden at the cool of the day, and they hid themselves the man and his wife from before the Lord God in the midst of the trees of the garden.

Nᴏᴛ only does sin involve an inward pollution and corruption of man's heart, but in addition, it involves guilt before God. When we say that a man is guilty before God what we mean is that he is liable to censure and to punishment from God. Realizing that God will punish them and rebuke them for what they have done Adam and Eve seek to hide from Him. The knowledge of good and evil, as they, fallen sinful creatures, now possessed it, awakened their conscience, and they knew that God is just and must punish sin. To hide from His presence seems the only thing to do.

What Adam and Eve hear is God's voice. This word would either mean the actual voice of God as He called aloud to them, or it might refer to the sound of the Lord as He approached the man and the woman in the garden. In favour of the first view is the fact that the Hebrew word which appears here normally means 'voice.' On the other hand, there are passages which show that the word may also mean 'sound.' In 2 Samuel 5:24, for example, 'And it shall be, when thou hearest the voice of a going in the tops of the mulberry trees . . . '. Here, without question the word 'voice' means 'sound.' So it is also in several other passages of the Bible. Hence, it may well be that what is meant here is that Adam and Eve heard the sound of the Lord as He walked in the garden. It is well not to be dogmatic.

In reading the verse in our English Bibles we may possibly think that it was the 'voice of God' which was walking. This, however, is not the meaning of the text. It is the Lord God who is walking. The word implies a walking about or to and fro. Hence, the thought of the verse is that the man and the woman heard the voice or sound of the Lord God as He was walking about in the garden. To state the matter simply: they heard the Lord God walking.

What, however, is meant when Scripture says that the Lord God was walking? Those who regard the chapter as a mere parable are not troubled by the problem. To them it is a mistake to consider the chapter as teaching what actually transpired. Rather the language constitutes what they would call an anthropomorphism, and they do not take it seriously. There are some however, who wish to take the Scripture more seriously. To them this chapter is not a parable at all. They would say that here is an anthropomorphism intended to teach that God is present with fallen man.

But is this a possible solution? We think not. If we are to take this chapter seriously, are we not compelled to recognize that it presents a conversation between God and man? How could this conversation have occurred, if God was not actually present in the garden in a form in which man could converse with Him? It is this fact of the conversation which rules out the idea that we have here only an anthropomorphic statement concerning God. How then shall we interpret what Scripture says?

God is the Infinite One; He is a spirit. In order to reveal Himself to man in an intimate way He appeared during Old Testament times in human form. Such appearances were called theophanies (appearances of God) and these theophanies found their culmination in the incarnation of the Second Person of the Trinity. We may thus speak of the theophanies as pre-incarnate appearances of the Lord. In most loving and tender condescension He appeared in the form of a man, so that He might speak to man as friend to friend. Throughout the Old Testament we read of such theophanies, until in the fulness of time God actually took to Himself human nature and became man, yet without sin.

So it would seem we must understand this appearance of the gracious Lord to Adam. When God created man He did not place him in a barren waste but prepared for him a garden, which man as God's guest was to preserve and keep. God is the owner of this garden, as He is of all the earth, and one of the blessings which unfallen man enjoyed was intimate converse with God the Creator. Man however, cannot speak face to face with a spirit; hence, God graciously appeared in human form so that man could speak directly to Him and receive from Him His commands. There is too great a wealth of detail in this narrative to dismiss the walking of God as a mere anthropomorphism. We are perhaps even warranted in assuming that God had often thus spoken with the man and woman. Formerly they would have rejoiced at the sound of His voice; because of sin, they now seek to hide themselves from Him, who has been good to them.

Scripture employs an interesting phrase to designate the time at which God was walking. In the English versions we read of the cool of the day. The word which these versions have rendered 'cool' is better translated by 'wind' or 'spirit.' Some think that the reference is to the morning wind, but this seems to be contrary to the word's usage. The phrase 'wind of the day' would be the time when a cool wind blew, toward evening. The definite article which appears in the phrase 'the day' suggests that the phenomenon was a familiar one. It is a beautiful description. Toward evening, late in the afternoon, the cool wind blows. Then it was that the Lord God was walking in the garden. But where are the ones whom He had created? They want no part of the scene, for they hear His voice and they hear it as His enemies.

Here begins the flight of fallen man from God; here begins man's attempt to do the impossible; here begins the effort to interpret life and reality apart from the Creator. Now man will face his own problems and, so he thinks, solve them—and all without God. Here begins the downward course that leads only to hell.

That the effort to hide from God was foolish hardly needs to be said. The trees of the garden were God's trees; had He not Himself planted them all? Was He not their Creator? How then could one of His creatures possibly hide from His presence? Yet is this attempt to hide from the Creator any more foolish than the efforts that fallen men constantly make to escape Him? Do not men today seek to suppress the knowledge of God?

Are they not ever trying to banish from their hearts any thoughts of Him? Do they not use device after device in an effort to avoid coming to grips with the realities of life? It is no more foolish to hide from God's presence in the midst of the trees of the garden than to espouse vigorously a philosophy of life which rules God out of the picture entirely.

Man was to have been the protector of the garden: now he desires the garden to protect him. As we read this verse we meet the words, 'in the midst of,' 'tree,' 'garden.' How often they have been used in this narrative! They constantly rise to confront us. It is as if the sinner was trying to forget his sin, but could not do so. At every step he encounters obstacles which remind him of the transgression which he has committed. It was a tree in the midst of the garden which had been connected with his fall; it was in the midst of the trees of the garden that he sought to hide from God. Wherever he may go, he is in God's territory. Whatever meets his eyes, points to God and claims Him as its Maker. This is God's world, and in it there is no escape from His presence. Indeed, there is but one way in which to flee from God, and that is to flee unto Him. Being in the darkness and ignorance of sin, however, Adam and Eve did not know this.

9. *And the Lord God called unto the man and he said unto him, Where art thou?*

MAN has broken away from God, but God will not leave him to his lost condition. Here appears the great marvel of the Scriptures; God does not abandon the creature to his just deserts. Had God stricken the man and the woman with instant physical and eternal death, no cry could have been raised against Him. It would be what man deserved, for God is of purer eyes than to behold evil. There is nothing that compels God to save man; He does so out of His own good pleasure, and His approach to man is in love.

How completely the meaning of this verse has been missed by those who think that God was seeking information as to Adam's whereabouts! That early antagonist of Christianity, Celsus, for example, thought that God called to Adam for the purpose of learning where Adam was. Celsus of course hated Christianity and sought to do all that he could to destroy it. He did not understand Christianity but that did not prevent him from making the most irresponsible charges against it. We may ever be thankful to God that He raised up so strong a warrior as Origen to refute the base charges of this opponent of revealed truth.

There have been those who think that the question was somewhat in the nature of a scolding, 'Now, Adam, where art thou? Look at the condition in which thou dost find thyself.' Others make of the question a cry of despair, 'Alas, now where art thou?' In the light of the subsequent procedure of God in announcing salvation it seems best to consider the question as designed to bring Adam to a realization of the nature of his condition and to a confession of his sin. It is the first blessed overture of saving grace in the Bible. In all justice God might have cast man then and there into everlasting punishment; instead He approached man in tender love to announce His determination to save him.

In this question God reveals His love, for the purpose of interrogating Adam is to cause him to see where his disobedience has brought him. It is as though God was saying, 'Where art thou now, Adam? What is this condition in which thou dost find thyself? Is this the knowledge that thou didst desire?' Through this gracious question, a question, we think, which is without reproach of Adam, the man must now look at himself. Has he attained to a knowledge that has brought to him a desirable condition of existence? Has he ascended to the plane of God and can he bask in the sunshine of comprehensive knowledge? Or, has his disobedience opened his eyes, so that he is able to see evil but is blind to the truth? Has he not received such an opening of the eyes that he really needs Christ who alone can open the eyes of the blind?

In that Adam's eyes are now opened, has he not actually become blind?

Scripture uses two verbs, God *called* and God *said*, but it is not two distinct acts of God to which reference is made. Rather, we might bring out the force of the verbs by paraphrasing, 'God called saying.' In calling out to Adam God is summoning him to the contemplation of his present status and possibly also to give an account of why he is in the condition in which he finds himself. It is to Adam that God first calls out, for Adam is the head of the wife and the primary responsibility rested upon him. God had prohibited Adam from partaking of the fruit of the tree of the knowledge of good and evil and so it was that God now in calling spoke to him. We may notice that the Bible expressly says, 'And God said to him': God's address was directed to Adam, the guilty one.

10. And he said, Thy voice I heard in the garden and I was afraid, for I was naked, and I hid myself.

Here is the voice of the sinner, and the sinner's voice is not straightforward, open and above board. Sin makes man a coward and an evader, it leads him to seek refuge in half truths, deceit and evasion. What Adam says is in part true, but it is hardly a manly statement. Adam is more concerned with the consequences of his sin than with the heinousness of what he had done. That he had disobeyed the good God who had so kindly given him the garden for his home does not trouble him. That he is naked, and so existing in unpleasant consequences does bother him. The sin and transgression are hidden behind the consequences. The awareness of his nakedness was more keenly in Adam's mind than the fact that he had broken God's command. Sin causes us to think more of what happens and will happen to us than of the fact that we have disobeyed God. Even in this respect it is deceptive. That we are in a miserable condition because of sin is sad indeed; that we have broken God's commands is heinous, and will lead to our complete punishment in everlasting death.

The first words of fallen man are words which set the

pattern as it were, for fallen mankind's continuing desire to suppress the knowledge of God and were it possible, to banish Him from thought. 'Thy voice,' says Adam, and those are the first words that he utters. The fall has not delivered man from God, as the serpent had hinted. What a temptation to think that by disobeying God and yielding to the serpent's suggestion one could be like God! No longer must one take his orders from God but can now have the same knowledge that God possessed. What a challenge that was! What a desirable goal to be attained!

But how deceiving were the tempter's words! In hearkening unto them Adam and his wife found no freedom at all from God, rather, His call reached unto them and they heard His voice. Even in their sinful condition they cannot escape from Him. Indeed, their sinful condition makes them desire to run away from Him. Yet this they cannot do. Wherever they cast their lot or turn their eyes, there He is to meet them. They are still His creatures, even though they have fallen into sin, and this is His world in which they live. Everything points to Him. The very garden through every tree, through every stone, through every particle of ground proclaims that God is its Maker, and that it belongs to Him. There is no escape from God.

God's voice sounds out, however, and summons Adam. He must respond, for God is his Maker. Gone however, are the joy and blessedness with which he once heard God's voice. The fellowship with his Creator is broken and is no more. God seeks him out in order to deal with his sin. Will God punish him? 'Thy voice,' he says; the voice which should have brought comfort now brings fear.

Upon hearing the voice of God Adam is afraid, and this fear he acknowledges. The reason for his fear is that he is naked, and he cannot appear naked before God. In his response to God Adam lays emphasis upon the word 'naked.' Inasmuch as he was naked, he declares, he hid himself. Of what, however, should he have been afraid? Is not God so loving that He is more eager to forgive man his sins than man is to be forgiven? Is not God so loving that He could never send a man to hell? Did not Adam know of the 'modern' discovery that all men are already reconciled to God and need only to be made aware of that fact? Was not Adam acting somewhat as a child? Is not God man's big brother who really exists for the service and pleasure of man? What a foolish thing to be afraid of God! What a childish thing to think that God might punish a sinner!

Adam, however, did not have the advantage of modern psychological views of religion; he was without the 'knowledge' that God exists only for man's glory. Adam had sinned, and he was afraid, and in being afraid he showed wisdom. He knew that he had sinned, and he was cognizant of the fact that what he had done was so serious that it invoked the displeasure of the Holy God. To Adam his sin was not now a light thing. He had no time for the easy-going interpretations of sin that modern psychology advances. He would have cast these things aside as 'rubbish,' for that is what they are. He was a sinner and he knew that he was guilty before God. His nakedness was to him a thing of shame and he dared not stand in God's presence. If it were at all possible he would hide himself from God's presence. To hide from God's presence, however, was impossible. Rather than face the holy God whom he feared, Adam attempts the impossible.

11. And he said, Who made known to thee that thou wast naked? is it that from the tree which I commanded thee not to eat, thou hast eaten?

PATIENTLY and in love God continues His questioning. Adam must be brought to a realization that the sin which he had committed was more serious than its consequences. He must have a deeper consciousness of his sin than of its effects, and graciously to awaken this consciousness God asks him a further question. He takes up the statement of Adam, namely that he was naked, and now asks who made this fact known to him. Well enough does God know who it was, but it is necessary that Adam also know who it was. To bring Adam to a true understanding He phrases His question in such a way that Adam will be compelled to answer it with the truth. Step by step therefore God elicits a confession from fallen Adam.

It is of interest to note that in His question God does not describe the tree. There is no need of that now. He speaks of it merely as 'the tree from which I commanded thee not to eat.' That is now the important point for Adam to take to heart. He has eaten from the tree from which God had commanded him not to eat. What must be impressed upon his mind is that in so eating he has dis-

84

obeyed God. This is more necessary than that at this juncture he be reminded that the tree was the tree of the knowledge of good and evil.

Not only must Adam come to a proper understanding of the nature of the serpent but he must also make a clean and honest acknowledgment of his transgression. Hence, the Lord's second question, 'Hast thou eaten?' requires a positive declaration that Adam has eaten. It is a straightforward question and it deserves a straightforward answer. God makes it easy for Adam to answer. A simple 'yes,' a simple acknowledgment would suffice. When David was confronted with his heinous sin against Bathsheba, he acknowledged, 'I have sinned against God.' That was all that Adam need do. 'I have sinned,' would have straightened the matter out. A simple honest confession, that was all that God sought.

12. *And the man said, The woman whom thou hast given to be with me; she gave to me from the tree and I ate.*

A SIMPLE, honest confession, how-
ever, was not forthcoming, for sin teaches the mind to be
devious and evasive. Adam was naked. Three times in
this context (i.e. verses 7-11) the word 'naked' is used.
Before God there now stands a man who is naked, who
realizes that he is naked and who looks upon that nakedness as something to be ashamed of. His sense of shame
had separated him from his wife so that he must clothe
himself and she herself, and the fact that they were naked
had caused them to seek to hide themselves from God's
presence. In itself nakedness is not a thing to be ashamed
of, but through his disobedience Adam's interpretation
of the nature of things had become perverted. Hence, in
his fallen condition he replies to God, but the reply is not
one that would do him credit.

Can a man who is naked and sinful give a just defence
of himself? Obviously he cannot, and Adam immediately
seeks to mitigate his guilt and to lessen the heinousness
of what he has done. The structure of this twelfth verse
is quite interesting, particularly with respect to the first
three words. We may bring this out as follows: 'And

VERSE 12

there said THE MAN THE WOMAN etc.' What is of interest is to notice the juxtaposition of the two words MAN and WOMAN. Each of the words has a definite article. Thus, in his reply to God, Adam first mentions the woman, and so emphasizes her. In so doing Adam seeks to lessen the gravity of his offence.

Here then is no manly confession but a vain attempt to shift blame. The woman gave Adam from the tree and he ate. As God had not described the tree in His question, but had merely spoken of 'the tree' so also Adam in his reply. It is simply the tree. There is no need now to remind oneself that it is the tree of the knowledge of good and evil. It is the tree, and the eating of the fruit of that tree which has caused the trouble. Adam knows well enough, all too well in fact, what tree it is.

Is not an evasive excuse also a weak one? It certainly is in this case. The fact that the woman gave Adam from the tree to eat is no reason why he should have eaten. Yet, Adam exhibits here a characteristic of fallen man. He is weak and allows himself easily to be led. Adam knew what was right, for the prohibition had been given to him directly. He should have led Eve, but allowed himself to be led of her. Thus, she who was created to be his help became the occasion of leading him into sin, and he who should have been her head yielded to her desire.

Fallen man all too easily yields to the will of others. For this reason false religions have their following; political demagogues can amass great groups of followers. Men allow themselves easily to become swayed, and not to resist the will of others, even when that will is sinful. Men who know better often give in to others' desires merely for the sake of expediency. Such yielding is sin, and it can never bring blessedness as its result. Adam is a fallen being; he is also a weak being; his courage has departed.

Flight from God leads to evasion and evasion leads to accusing others. And when we have taken refuge in accusing others we often become bold and brazen in our sin. Not only was it the woman who gave Adam from the tree, but it was 'the woman whom thou gavest me.' Thus Adam seeks to shift the blame from himself to God. The implication is clear enough. 'If Thou hadst not given me the woman, this act would not have taken place.' This is reckless, brazen effrontery, and it is deceitful and untruthful. God had indeed given Adam the woman, but Adam himself knew who she was and why she was created. He had declared that she was bone of his bone and flesh of his flesh. Well enough did he know that she had been taken from himself, and that she was essentially one with him. Although the animals were helps, no one of them was a help that was meet for him. Only the woman fulfilled that role. To accuse God therefore of having given him 'the woman' as though she were something strange and essentially other than he was, was unjust in the extreme. God had given Adam the woman, but she was given to be a help. What God had designed to be a blessing and a help for Adam so that he would not live alone, is rejected and God is accused of having in a sense been responsible for the sad thing that has taken place.

Thus Adam seeks to exonerate himself, and this he does in an unpraiseworthy manner. His words are also divisive. In partaking of the forbidden fruit the man and his wife had been together. The community of action, however, is now broken, for sin separates men and divides them one from another. In his first utterance (verse 10) fallen man acknowledges the consequences of his sin. In his second utterance (verse 12) he casts blame upon his wife. Thus sin wrought its divisive action even in our first parents.

Is not the lesson to be learned all too apparent? It is useless to talk of men solving their own problems, as long as they are sinners, for in its very nature sin tends to divide men and to make them hate one another. When we see racial hatred it is because there is hatred in the human heart. The vicious tensions of our modern day cannot be solved by legislation. Until something is done to change the heart, there can be no hope. Man the sinner is essentially selfish, looking out first of all for his own desires and well being. He acts as did his father Adam. Hence, the more one ponders the problems of modern society, the more one realizes that basically they stem from the fact that man is a sinner. Can these problems be solved by man? The answer is a resounding negative. Only a superficial optimism would believe that man in himself can remove the tensions of modern society. The more profoundly one surveys the present scene, the more does one come to realize that the hope of the world lies not in many acts of fallen man, nor in some supposed gradual progress of modern society but simply and solely in one redemptive act of the Lord Himself.

Finally, Adam acknowledges that he ate. These are the last words of the verse, but they constitute a disgraceful confession. Having supposedly shifted the blame to Eve and ultimately to God, there is nothing to preclude Adam from at last acknowledging that he has disobeyed God. Here is no confession of a broken and penitent heart; rather it is almost a bold challenge. 'Of course I ate. I acted as a responsible thinking person. I am not going to be bound by an authority which is questionable. On the best of authority I have learned that the fruit of this tree will make me wise, and there is nothing wrong in the pursuit of wisdom. Let me follow the great goal of obtaining knowledge from all sources whatever. No narrow presuppositions or prejudices bind me. I am free. If the fact that I ate displeases Thee, Thou Thyself gavest this woman to me, and she gave me of the tree. Of course I ate.' Twice Adam uses the word 'gave,'—a word which suggests that God had set or appointed the woman to be at Adam's side. Others were the cause of the trouble, he implies: God gave the woman, and the woman gave the fruit.

13. And the Lord God said to the woman, What is this thou hast done, and the woman said, The serpent beguiled me, and I ate.

*A*DAM'S statement is not worthy of a reply, and God does not deign to answer it. As it were He cuts Adam off, and simply turns to the woman. We have said that sin had divided mankind, and this is true. Adam betrayed his wife and separated himself from her. He had no desire to defend her, but would allow her to stand as it were upon her own two feet. At the same time, despite the divisive nature of sin, there is a certain solidarity which sin brings to the human race, namely, that all men are involved in sin and all are guilty before God. Like Adam, Eve too must now hear God's questioning. Like Adam she too is responsible to Him and must give an account unto Him of her actions.

How patiently God deals with her! Yet she must stand alone, for sin renders men lonely. God need not hear the woman, but does so only out of love. He wills to bring both Eve and her husband to a confession of their sin and to a realization of the heinousness of what they have done. His question, 'What now hast thou done?' or 'What is this thou hast done?' is of course not an effort to obtain information. Well enough does He know what she has done, but in so questioning her He may bring her also to the awareness of her action.

Like Adam Eve has little or no concern over her guilt. Her main object is to shift the blame from herself and so to suggest that after all her action was not so heinous. Hence she mentions the serpent, and in this mention we have a problem. Adam had accused God of giving him the woman but Eve does not say a word about how the serpent came into the garden. And where the Bible is silent, we may follow its example. Not a word is said in the Bible as to the precise time of Satan's creation. What is primarily important for us to remember is that he is but a creature; he is not co-eternal with God. We should probably place his creation somewhere within the six days of Genesis one, although exactly where one cannot say. That he was created before man is probably a warranted supposition.

When Satan rebelled against God and entered the garden we do not know. For that matter we do not know how long man lived in the garden before he disobeyed God. Sometime after Adam was placed in Eden Satan entered the garden and took possession of a serpent, using it as his instrument. This we must assume, although the Scripture does not state this in so many words.

Of these things Eve evidently knows nothing. Her contacts had been only with the serpent, for she had seen only him. Hence, she says nothing about the origin of the serpent nor about how he came to be in the garden. Doubtless, she had seen serpents many times before, but when this one particular serpent began to speak, she had her first contact with evil.

At any rate she merely speaks of the serpent as a beast which is well known and assumes that God knows what serpent she is referring to. This serpent beguiled her. Thus also is the divine interpretation given in 2 Corinthians 11:3, 'But I fear, lest by any means, as the serpent deceived Eve through his subtilty, so your minds should be corrupted from the simplicity that is in Christ.' The Hebrew verb simply means 'to deceive.' Eve is at least aware of the fact that she has been deceived. The outcome is not what she had expected. Looking for wisdom, she had found ignorance. The tree had been deceptive, for she had seen it as pleasant to the eyes and good for food, but now she stood naked before God, condemned.

Again we have the striking order of statement that appeared also in Adam's words. 'And there said THE WOMAN THE SERPENT.' Thus Eve places the words *the woman* and *the serpent* together. It is 'THE SERPENT' which brings the issue out in the open. God does not give the serpent an opportunity to speak but addresses him directly

14. And the Lord God said to the serpent, Because thou hast done this, Cursed art thou above all cattle and above all beasts of the field; upon thy belly thou shalt go, and dust thou shalt eat all the days of thy life.

GOD asks the serpent no questions, for the serpent has no right to speak before God. To the man and his wife God intends to show mercy, but not to that power which has used the serpent. The serpent therefore receives his due rebuke and judgment. It is the consistent teaching of the Bible that sin deserves punishment. The absolute justice of God requires that the sinner be punished for his transgressions. Punishment, therefore, is not for the purpose of reforming the sinner but to vindicate and satisfy the absolute justice of a Holy God. Nor is punishment properly conceived as the natural process which man's sinful acts sets in motion. It is not merely the unhappy consequence that follows upon man's sin, but is rather a judicial penalty which God's judgment inflicts.

How often we are told that sin brings with it its own punishment! Let a man do some evil deed, and the consequences of that deed are its punishment. Man makes his own hell upon this earth. This false doctrine is widely proclaimed, but it is not the teaching of Holy Scripture. True enough, evil deeds bring their unpleasant consequences with them, and these consequences, stemming from evil, are indeed unhappy. But punishment, according to the Bible, belongs to the moral realm. It is that which God decrees shall be visited upon the sinner. In the questions of God directed to Adam and Eve we hear God speak as the absolutely righteous One, and in the curse which He pronounces upon the serpent, we behold His holy justice at work!

How can one speak to a serpent? Here again we face the difficulty that arises from the fact that the serpent speaks. To address a serpent is to assume that the serpent is a rational, responsible being. We must assume then, that the Lord God, in speaking to the serpent is addressing the beast as the instrument of the evil one, and that the words spoken to the serpent strike home at this evil one, the tempter of mankind.

The language, 'because thou hast done this' suggests that the serpent was a responsible being. Actually, of course, a mere snake, inasmuch as it is not a rational creature, cannot be held accountable for what it does. The purpose of the curse pronounced upon the serpent is to make clear that there had been a deep-seated wickedness using it, and so the curse of a perpetual degradation was a forerunner of that eternal reproach which was to come upon the one who had used the serpent. The very fact of the pronouncing of a curse in itself makes clear that a higher, spiritual power was involved. The condemnation placed upon the serpent is in line with the principle whereby an animal which had been used in an unnatural crime was to be put to death. It is thus, for example, that we are to understand the language of Genesis 9:5, 'And surely your blood of your lives will I require; at the hand of every beast will I require it, and at the hand of man; at the hand of every man's brother will I require the life of man.' Other passages in the Bible illustrate the same point. A beast which had injured a man was ordered to be put to death and any beast which had participated in an unnatural crime with man was along with the man also to be killed. Of course the beast in such cases was not accountable nor responsible, yet it had been used by man and so was under his power to be employed in an unnatural purpose. As therefore the penalty of death came upon man so also it was meted out to the beast which man had subdued for unholy ends.

How can one curse a serpent? This creature which is not responsible will not be able to respond intellectually to the declaration that it must crawl upon its belly. Does the serpent feel any degradation in that it goes upon its belly? Obviously such is not the case. What is spoken in verse fourteen seems to place its emphasis upon the actual serpent which had spoken to Eve, and the punishment which fell upon the serpent was really a symbol of the deeper punishment to strike the evil one.

'According to the greatness of the serpent, so was his downfall,' reads a statement in the Talmud, 'because he was cunning ABOVE ALL, he is cursed ABOVE ALL.' Perhaps there is a word play between 'cursed' (ah-room) and 'naked' (ay-rohm). In the previous verses the word 'naked' had been prominent. There the background was that of the consequences of sin. Here it is the curse which comes to the foreground. Man had been concerned about the sad results of his action. Now, however, he must learn that God's justice is to be manifested, and this justice is shown in the curses which are pronounced.

God curses the serpent 'away from' the cattle and beasts of the earth. The thought is not that of comparison, as though the Lord had said that all the beasts would be cursed, but that the serpent would be cursed more than any. Rather, in the curse the serpent is separated from the other beasts. Whereas they are free, he is now in a peculiar bondage. Upon him alone of all the beasts does God pronounce the curse, for he alone had tempted the woman.

It is true that the whole creation is under bondage and groaneth and travaileth together, as the apostle says in Romans 8; but this is not the curse mentioned here. The creation is in bondage because of man's sin; it was man himself who plunged the whole creation into bondage, not the serpent. In this curse the serpent stands alone and unique, and in this curse he is separated from the animals. He of all the animals receives the curse, whether they be the tame animals or the wild beasts which roam the fields.

The essence of the curse is stated simply in the words that the serpent will go upon his belly and eat dust. Here is the language of deep degradation, and the meaning is that in the eyes of man the serpent will from henceforth be despised. But did the serpent always go upon his belly? Did he always crawl along in the tortuous manner that we now see? There are those who think that before the fall he was upright, and that he walked upright. It was the fall, so they hold, which brought about an actual change in his mode of locomotion. Before the fall, we are told, the entire animal world was different from what it is now, and so the serpent must have undergone a great change. It also must have been bright and attractive so that it would have drawn Eve's attention. This may be but we must remember that the Bible is written for men who live after the fall took place and after man was driven from Eden. When therefore, the Bible speaks of a serpent, we bring to mind only the reptile which we know. We know no serpents but those which crawl about in what seems to us a tortuous fashion. If before the fall the serpent possessed some other mode of locomotion, we do not know that fact, and there is really nothing in the Scripture to indicate it.

In the eyes of man the repulsive manner in which the serpent crawls is his punishment. 'Whatsoever goeth upon the belly, and whatsoever goeth upon all four, or whatsoever hath more feet among all creeping things that creep upon the earth, them ye shall not eat; for they are an abomination.' (Leviticus 11:42). Into this class of abominable things the serpent is to be cast.

Likewise the eating of dust is not necessarily to be understood as referring to the serpent's food, but is a phrase expressing the deepest degradation. It may be that in crawling in the dust the serpent swallows dust, but this is not necessarily implied. As a result of this curse the serpent becomes a despised and hated object in the eyes of mankind, and in a certain sense we may say that in the serpent we see Satan. Satan has become the object of abhorrence upon man's part.

Similar in import are the expressions of other passages of Scripture. 'They shall lick the dust like a serpent,' writes Micah (7:17), 'they shall move out of their holes like worms of the earth; they shall be afraid of the Lord our God, and shall fear because of thee.' Micah's strong expression merely means that men shall fall to the ground in death, not that they will actually lick the dust. His language is derived from the act of the serpent in sticking out its tongue as it crawls. In a similar vein the Psalmist declares, 'They that dwell in the wilderness shall bow before him; and his enemies shall lick the dust.' It is an expression which we have adopted into our own language.

In the early days of the Christian Church there was a sect, known as the Ophites. This was not a Christian sect, but rather, as its name implies, one which worshipped the devil. Ophis is the Greek word for serpent. It is not strange that the symbol of this sect was the snake. Yet the people worshipped not the snake but the devil, or possibly the devil in the form of a snake. Likewise, in fairly recent times there were the Yezidee devil-worshippers in the Druze mountains of Syria, who, like the Ophites of old, worshipped the devil, and their emblem was the serpent. This is a perversion and a deep wickedness, for it is calling good what God has cursed.

Perhaps there is a reason for the mention of eating the dust. It was in the matter of eating that the tempter had caused the woman to fall. To eat the fruit of the tree of the knowledge of good and evil was presented to her as something greatly to be desired. In the curse, therefore, the serpent will also eat, and his eating the dust will be a reminder of that eating for which he was once responsible. To declare, as some have done, that serpents do not eat dust, and that for that reason Genesis is unscientific is to miss the point of the language.

Should it not likewise be apparent that the purpose of this account is not merely to explain the antipathy that exists between mankind and the serpents? Men do possess an antipathy toward snakes, but surely there is present here a deeper meaning than merely to explain the origin of that antipathy. What would be the purpose of the Bible in giving such an explanation? Why should mankind know what the origin of such antipathy was? If the purpose is simply to tell us why serpents crawl, then have we not a right to ask why the Bible does not tell why dogs bark and are friendly to men, why birds fly in the air or fish swim in the sea?

Such explanations as these are really trifling, and do not come to grips with the great seriousness found in the chapter. The tragic condition of mankind and his estrangement from God are consequences of the serpent's act. To overlook this and to see in the account nothing more than an ancient attempt to explain the reason why men dislike snakes is to trifle with one of the most profound documents ever written.

We must note briefly the final words of the verse, 'all the days of thy life.' The language does not mean that this particular snake alone in distinction from other snakes will crawl upon its belly all its life. Rather, the language applies to all snakes. It was the snake which tempted the woman; it is the serpent brood which in man's eyes will always be degraded. 'The serpent is thus,' writes Hengstenberg, 'by its disgusting form, and by the degradation of its whole being, doomed to be the visible representative of the kingdom of darkness, and of its head, to whom it had served as an instrument.' By tempting man the evil one thought to enlarge his kingdom and the scope of his rule. In a certain sense he does this, but in the eyes of the one whom he has harmed he is despised and must ever go on his belly. A perpetual and disgusting end!

15. And enmity will I place between thee and the woman and between thy seed and her seed, he will bruise thee as to the head and thou wilt bruise him as to the heel.

Almost imperceptibly the language passes from the actual serpent to address the evil one who has used the serpent. In verse fourteen the serpent had been in the foreground, and in the present verse the tempter himself appears. What had been uttered in the preceding verse did indeed also refer to the tempter; in the disgusting degradation that God imposed upon the serpent the tempter also was involved. Of all creatures—for Satan is only a creature, despite his pretensions to be otherwise—Satan is the most revolting and disgusting. No glorious king is he but only a prince and father of liars, who, knowing that his doom is sure, goes about like a roaring lion—without possessing the majesty of the lion—seeking whom he may devour.

We do well to note, however, that God is in control of the situation. How boastful the tempter had been! Without hesitation he had promised the woman freedom from God's commands. In doing this he did not show much originality. This is to be expected, for Satan is not original. The old 'line' which he used on Eve in Eden is the same one that his followers have constantly been repeating. Satan is not sufficiently clever to think up a new approach, although he delights in ringing the changes upon the word 'new.' Strong indeed are the vials of scorn which he pours out upon certain words, 'tradition,' 'doctrine,' 'law,' 'authority' and the like. In their place he overworks his favourite words and phrases, 'new,' 'unprejudiced,' 'disinterested search for truth,' 'freedom from intellectual bondage,' and the like. Hence, his thought had appeared very tempting to Eve. Here was the opportunity for her to enlarge her personality, to obtain the freedom necessary to give full expression to her own potential, to break the bonds of public opinion and especially the shackles of religion. In breaking away from God, she thought she could obtain true freedom.

This was the first time that the tempter had used this approach on a human being. But Satan has kept at it ever since, and all too willingly the sinful heart of man, already prejudiced in his favour, has listened to him. Had he not spoken as God? Indeed, had he not even exalted himself above God? Did he not give to Eve the impression that his word was true and the word of God was false?

How strange then that the tempter must listen to the curse pronounced upon himself by God? Where now are his power and his wisdom? Where now is the daring which led him to raise himself above the Creator of all things? He says not a word for he is in the presence of the righteous Judge of all the earth. Satan listens as the curse is pronounced. And what a blessing for mankind that the tempter must listen to God! What comfort we may derive from this fact!

There is only One that can overcome the tempter; only One who can cause him to be silent and to listen, and that is God. We may sometimes fall into the error of thinking that Satan is on an equality with God. Well is it, then, that we bring to mind that Satan is but a creature. He may be wiser than we, but his wisdom is devilish, and he is not all wise. Only God is all wise. The evil one may have and does have far more power than we, but he is not omnipotent. Only God possesses all power. With a rapidity that is like lightning Satan may travel about to execute his wicked designs, but Satan is localized; he cannot be in more than one place at a time. He is a creature both of space and time; God alone is omnipresent. Satan the creature is no match for God the Creator. When the evil of the world overwhelms us, may we remember this. Our God can cause the evil one to listen and can pronounce righteous condemnation upon the adversary of men's souls.

> *Fear not, O little flock, the foe*
> *Who madly seeks your overthrow;*
> *Dread not his rage and power:*
> *What though your courage sometimes faints,*
> *His seeming triumph o'er God's saints*
> *Lasts but a little hour.*
>
> *As true as God's own Word is true,*
> *Nor earth nor hell with all their crew*
> *Against us shall prevail.*
> *A jest and byword are they grown;*
> *God is with us, we are his own;*
> *Our victory cannot fail.*

For Satan it is the most humiliating moment of his existence hitherto, for he hears his doom pronounced in words of infallible authority. Or does he? May it not be that we are completely mistaken in interpreting this chapter of Satan and the fall of man? A modern objection to such an interpretation goes somewhat as follows. The early Christian fathers, it is said, applied this verse to Christ and even labelled it the 'Protevangelium,' or the first preaching of the Gospel. We know, however, as a result of scientific study that this is not the sense of the passage. Actually there is no Messianic prophecy here, and so, of course, there is no reference at all to Satan. Possibly, however, the writer, whoever he was (modern negative criticism seems to be assured that he was not Moses) had some kind of an inkling that the passage did after all have something to do with man's redemption. Of course, this writer did not see Christ here and he did not see Satan, but he may have sensed that there was more here than meets the eye. In writing down this verse he probably was using an old tradition which he himself did not fully understand.

Not all modern critics would agree with such a statement of the case, but there is an almost universal consensus that this is not a Messianic prophecy. Our answer to this position will, we hope, become clearer, as we proceed. At present it may indeed be well to point out the uniqueness of this verse. In all the literature of antiquity there is nothing which even remotely resembles it; it stands completely alone. We here face a condemnation uttered against a tempter who had brought about the fall of man into sin. This tempter had led the woman and the man to an estrangement from God. Their act was moral, and wholly divorced from the realm of magic. As a result of what Adam did, mankind was plunged into a state of sin.

This moral state was not merely one of unhappiness and unpleasantness for man. It was that, but it was far more. It was an estate in which man no longer enjoyed communion with his God. God withdrew from man His favour and the light of His countenance, for man was guilty before Him. And this guilt demanded punishment. We do not rightly read these verses of Genesis unless we see that in the pronouncement of the curses, God is acting as a righteous Judge. This estate into which mankind had fallen was one that may be characterized by the word 'death.' Man in his trespasses and sins was dead, and desperately in need of life. It is to promise life to man that the words of this verse are uttered, and such life can come from God alone. In the broadest sense of the term, therefore, this is a proclamation of good news, an announcement to sinful fallen man that God will do something to bring blessing to him. Despite all that negative criticism has written to the contrary, and it has written plenty, we would affirm, for all the evidence supports us, that this is a preaching of the Gospel.

Did Luther go too far when he said, 'This text embraces and contains within itself everything noble and glorious that is to be found anywhere else in the Scriptures?' Perhaps he did; it is a strong statement, possibly an extreme one, but it points to the truth that the heart of the Biblical message is found in this verse. And the heart of that message is redemption. Redemption it is which we have here. In a position of emphasis, standing at the beginning of the verse as we read it in the Hebrew, is the word 'enmity.' That word overshadows all else and sets the tone for the entire verse. It expresses the very essence, as it were, of the deliverance which God is declaring to mankind.

Enmity! But was there not enmity already present? Had not man shown an enmity, even an hostility toward God when he had partaken of the forbidden fruit? Had he not also, in a certain way, displayed an enmity toward his wife, when he sought to shift the blame to her? How then can there be anything praiseworthy in the introduction of more enmity? Why is such prominence given to this word?

It is true that there had been enmity present before this promise was made, but it had been the wrong kind of enmity. Man had hated, but he had hated the wrong object. He had been at enmity, but his own enmity was turned toward God, whereas toward God he should have exhibited love and delight. To exhibit enmity toward God is also to manifest the fact that one is a fallen, depraved creature. In the deepest and most true sense of the word it may be said that no right thinking person will hate God or be at enmity with Him. To be at enmity with God therefore is to show that one is not right thinking. And when man is a fallen creature he is not a right thinking creature. He needs above all else a complete reversal of all his values. He must learn to hate what formerly he loved, and he must learn to love what formerly he hated.

Adam had been at enmity and hence had acted from a wrong perspective. His sense of values had been wholly perverted; in all his thoughts he judged from a point of view that was basically contrary to the truth. And his fallen descendants are like him. Inasmuch as their outlook on the entirety of life proceeds from a perverted point of view they basically misjudge everything. Is this not the explanation of the fact that men seem to call that good which is evil and that evil which is good? Does not man deceive himself into thinking that the evil is the normal, and the good too confining and restraining? Whence comes this hatred of law and authority and the supposed interest in man's 'freedom' to express himself as he will but from a heart that is deeply at enmity with God?

Indeed Adam had been at enmity, but if he is to be delivered from his lost condition—and his condition in every sense of the word was a lost one—he must learn who his true enemy is. He must learn that what he needs is something so all-embracing and revolutionary that a complete change of viewpoint is demanded. Adam's loyalties must undergo a radical transformation. Enmity in itself is not to be abandoned; he is not to become a flabby, lifeless creature without enmity. But Adam must have a rightly-directed enmity. There are some objects which he must abhor and against which he must stand. To be at enmity with the wrong object is to lose one's life. To be at enmity with the right object is to be delivered. Not God, but the serpent is the object to be hated. Unless Adam and Eve come to realize that God is their friend and the serpent their enemy, they will be basically mistaken about all things and in a fundamental sense will misjudge all things.

Although he probably thought that his actions hitherto had been most commendable, they had actually been reprehensible. Had not Adam and Eve however, engaged in a disinterested search for knowledge and truth? Had they not been bold enough to exhibit their 'freedom' even from God's commands? Had they not striven, in the best style of the modern existentialist philosopher or the protesting college student, to manifest a whole hearted devotion to their own personalities and a rebellion against traditional authority? What more could be demanded of them? And yet the way they chose, so seemingly praiseworthy, is, as this way always is, the way of death. No, it was not a disinterested search for truth at all; it was a path that was founded upon bias and prejudice; it bristled with presuppositions. It was a way that was in harmony with the dictates of the father of lies and that could lead to a 'truth' in which the holy God was not needed. The 'knowledge' after which rebellious Adam sought was a knowledge of things in which God had no part. It was a sad way, for no matter how noble and praiseworthy fallen man may assert that it is, the way of disobedience to God's commands leads, as with Adam, unto everlasting death.

Adam, therefore, to put it simply, needed a change of heart. And this was to be no mere superficial reversal of one's mind; it was far deeper than that. According to the New Testament, it was something so radical that it could be labelled a new birth. The old Adam must go; he was in the way of death; there must be a new Adam, an Adam who will love what he should love and hate what he should hate.

If Adam must then learn to hate the serpent and to be

at enmity with him, he must also learn to love God. God had all along been his friend, and the tempter his enemy, but Adam, inasmuch as his own heart was darkened by sin did not recognize the true state of affairs. He had misjudged things about as completely as one can misjudge them. Had he not looked upon God as an enemy? Had he not been perfectly willing to go along with his wife? And had he not looked upon the serpent as his friend? Does not this explain why he together with his wife was ready and willing to listen to the words of the tempter and to ignore the words of God?

If then Adam is to learn to love God there must be a complete reversal of his attitude. If he is to love God he must obey God and must realize that in disobeying God he had done a despicable thing. All talk of freedom from constraints, of searching for truth, of the goal of comprehensive knowledge and the like must be swept away and discarded as the rubbish that it really is. Disobedience to God, no matter what high-sounding language may cover it, is despicable and heinous. It must be rejected completely. It is an evidence of hatred toward God and love of evil; obedience to God is on the other hand a token or pledge of love to Him. A great change was necessary, and this change must take place in Adam and Eve.

On the part of the serpent there is to be no change. He had been no friend of man, and his pretended friendliness and interest were but a mask. He is man's arch enemy. His chief delight would be in man's destruction for therein he thinks that he can thwart the purpose of the blessed One whom he most hates. The tempter will continue breathing out hatred, for he is a god of hatred. He hates God and he hates man. His purpose is to confound and to destroy, to pervert and to overturn.

Man, however, must be at enmity with the serpent. God does not advise man to be at enmity with the serpent, for man would not have the power to follow that advice. Nor does God command man to hate the evil one. Such commands would place upon man a responsibility which he could not discharge. He could not discharge it for to do so would be to act as one that was spiritually alive and had the power to obey such a command. Man, however, did not have the power or strength to yield such obedience, for, through his first act of disobedience he had fallen into an estate of sin and misery. In his trespasses and sins he was dead, and one who is dead is unable to act as one who is alive.

Had God uttered to man the command to be at enmity with the serpent, He would have had every right to do so, even though man would have had no power to obey. God would have been just, had He so commanded, but how sad for fallen man! That God did not issue such a command is one of the most wonderful facts of the Bible. Of course, whether God had issued such a command or not, man's responsibility is to be at enmity with the evil one and to love God. But to have issued such a command at this particular time would simply have pointed out more clearly how utterly hopeless man was in his lost estate.

Instead of so commanding, God gives a glorious indicative in which He announces what His intentions are. 'I will place,' He says, and in these simple words there flows forth all the triumphant riches of His saving, sovereign grace. God takes the initiative, for this He must do if man is to be delivered. If God does not act, there can be no hope. In the Hebrew there is an alliteration between the word 'enmity' (ayvah) and 'I will place' (ahshith), an alliteration which helps one to keep these two words (for in Hebrew there are but two words) clearly in mind.

There is danger that we overlook the force of the Lord's declaration. He does not say merely that He will stir up and bring to life an enmity that is already present, but merely slumbering. It is not an arousing of enmity from slumber that God will instigate. Nor is it a promoting of enmity between the woman and the serpent. Rather, it is a placing of enmity between the woman and the serpent. The enmity is not now present at the time when God speaks but must be placed there by God. The woman cannot place it there, but God can, and it is that which He declares He will do. He will place or put this enmity between the woman and the serpent. What does not now exist He will Himself bring into existence, for He is the God of power. Only God can do what must be done if man is to be delivered, and this He graciously announces He will do.

Does this enmity cease with the death of the woman? Were this a mere legend or parable, nothing more than a story from ancient time, one might suspect that such would be the case. This enmity, however, is to be continuous; it is to extend both to the seed of the woman and of the serpent. Just as the woman is to be at enmity with the serpent, so also will her seed and the seed of the serpent be enemies. What, however, is meant by the woman's seed? Does it refer to one individual or does it refer to all who have descended from Eve? In the early Christian Church there were many who believed that there was here a specific reference to Jesus Christ as the Seed of the woman. It is of course true that Jesus Christ is the 'Seed' who has wrought the victory over Satan, but is that the sense of the language in this verse?

For one thing, it seems strange to assume that the enmity which God has placed between the woman and Satan is to extend only to one Descendant. The very nature of the language suggests that by the word 'seed' the entire body of Eve's descendants is intended. Furthermore, it is clear that the seed of the serpent is not one individual, but is to be understood in a collective sense as including all who descend from the serpent. Nor is it beside the point to note that in verse 16, the Lord speaks of the woman bringing forth sons. In this verse, it is made clear that there is to be more than one descendant of the woman. This statement clearly suggests that in verse fifteen also more than one individual is intended.

Another point should be noted. In the Old Testament there is a remarkable progression in God's revelation of the truth concerning the Messiah. As we turn over the pages of the Old Testament, examining one after another the Messianic prophecies, we are struck by the strange manner in which God progressively reveals more and more concerning the Person of the One whom He is to send into the world to heal the breach between Himself and the fallen human race. This is particularly noteworthy in the Pentateuch. In the first five books of the

Old Testament, there is a gradual unfolding of God's truth concerning the Messiah. At first we are told only in a general way that salvation is to come, and then step by step the identity of the Redeemer is brought into the foreground. In the eighteenth chapter of Deuteronomy, which is the last Messianic prophecy in the Pentateuch, we are told that there will be a 'prophet like unto Moses,' yet even in this prophecy, the person of the Messiah appears in what we may call a veiled form. Indeed, it is not until we come to the great prophecy of Isaiah that we have a clear cut revelation of His Person.

In Genesis as we proceed from prophecy to prophecy we do learn that salvation is to be through Abraham, and then furthermore we learn that it will be through Isaac rather than Ishmael. As we close the book of Genesis we have the knowledge that we are to look to the tribe of Judah for the coming Redeemer. Yet only dimly, as it were, do we see Him. We do see Him, but not with the clear light of fulfilment that characterizes the pages of the New Testament. Inasmuch as this is so, it would be very strange to find here in the first of all the prophecies which point to the coming salvation a clear-cut presentation of a personal Messiah. Were such the case this utterance would then go far beyond many of the later Messianic prophecies. In this one consideration, we think, there is a strong argument for not regarding this verse as presenting in any clear-cut way a personal Messiah. By the 'seed of the woman,' then, we are to understand, not a personal Messiah, but the entire human race.

If then the seed of the woman is the entirety of her

descendants what are we to understand by the seed of the serpent? Some think that it refers to fallen human beings who align themselves upon the serpent's side in opposition to God. It is of course true that our Lord said to the Pharisees, 'Ye are of your father the devil.' Men who oppose the kingdom of God and take their stand upon Satan's side, according to this interpretation, are the seed of the serpent. It is true, in a certain sense, that they are such. The Pharisees were the seed of the devil, and so are all men who serve the devil and hate the Lord. Although there is then a certain sense in which this is true, is this, however, what is intended by the present verse? Does this verse mean to suggest that the seed of the woman is the entire human race, whereas the seed of the serpent is that part of the fallen human race which is not to be saved, but remains on the devil's side?

One strong objection to such an understanding of the verse is that it would then include some people in the category of the woman's seed and also in that of the seed of the serpent. Those who hate God, while being the seed of Eve, would nevertheless, at the same time also be the serpent's seed, and the verse seems to suggest that there is an enmity between the two seeds. How could this be if men were both the seed of the woman and of the serpent? This interpretation, therefore, seems to go contrary to what is intended by the language of the text.

Is it not more in keeping with what the language of the text seems to require to look for the seed of the serpent outside the realm of the human race? If the woman's seed is mankind, and there is to be enmity between mankind and the serpent's seed, would it not seem that the serpent's seed was something other than mankind? Far better, therefore, because in keeping with the demands of the Scripture at this point is it to hold that the serpent's seed is found in evil spirits. These are his spiritual seed, not descended from him in a physical sense, but nevertheless, truly his seed. Satan rules over a kingdom of evil which is opposed to God, and this kingdom of evil is his seed. Between this seed of Satan and mankind there is to be enmity.

What is the nature of this enmity between the human kind and the kingdom of evil? Is it merely passive, or does it break forth into active hostility? Our text leaves us in no doubt as to the answer. 'He will bruise thy head,' we read in our English Bibles. Some students of the Bible, however, think that this is not a satisfactory rendering of the Hebrew verb. That verb, they tell us, cannot really be rendered satisfactorily in English. Apparently, they think, there is a word play between two rather similar sounding roots in the Hebrew. One of these means to 'snap after,' and then 'to pant after' or 'to lie in wait for.' But this causes a difficulty. If the verb means 'to lie in wait for,' then, whereas it may apply well to the action of the serpent, it does not fit well with the action of the woman's seed. On the other hand, it is held, if the verb means 'to bruise,' that may be in order when we speak of the action of the woman's seed, but what about the serpent's seed? How can he be said to bruise the heel of the seed of the woman? As a result there are those who think that in the first instance we should translate by 'bruise,' and read, 'he will bruise thy head,' and then in the second, 'and thou shalt lay in wait for his heel.' This is a possibility but it is rather unlikely. It would seem that the word should have the same significance in both instances. This is supported by the similar spelling of the word, which we may represent for the English reader as follows: y͏ᵉshuf͏ᵉka and t͏ᵉshufennu.

This is not the place to bring before the reader a technical discussion of the problem. We shall therefore, simply translate the verse as it is done in the English versions. 'He shall bruise thy head and thou shalt bruise his heel.' Nor is this translation without meaning. What is meant is that the seed of the woman will deliver a capital blow, whereas the serpent for his part will deliver a lesser blow. The words head and heel are quite interesting, and we may bring out their force in the sentence by rendering, 'as to the head' and 'as to the heel.' In other words, they show in what respect the injury is to be inflicted. The seed of the woman strikes a capital blow, whereas the serpent gives but a lesser one. All that the serpent can do is lie in wait for the man and bite him on the heel, which, pernicious and painful as it may be, is not the same as the capital blow which man himself can deliver. Walking upright, man can trample upon the head of the serpent and so destroy him. Crawling upon its belly in the dust, the serpent cannot inflict a decisive blow. Having been cursed by God so to crawl, the serpent receives in this very mode of locomotion a sign of his sure defeat.

Is it not apparent, however, from the very context, that something more is intended than that at some time in the future a serpent will bite a man? In speaking to the serpent God says, 'Thou shalt bruise his heel.' It is the serpent himself and not his seed which is to bruise the seed of the woman. Does not this mean that this particular serpent will live on and so bruise the heel of one of the descendants of the woman? To ask this question is to bring to the light the fact that more is involved than an actual serpent. The serpent that tempted Eve no doubt died thereafter in the ordinary course of events. But the very language is evidence that God is speaking to one more powerful than a serpent; the one who used the serpent for his evil purposes. To place enmity between the serpent and the woman is to point to something higher than a snake, for how can a mere snake be at enmity with a human being?

In the original creation God had placed man over the animals and in the promised redemption man is again to be above the animals in that he will subdue them. The blow which mankind will deliver will show the superiority of the human race over the lower animals and will re-instate the original divinely-imposed order. In this victory not only will the animal be returned to its rightful position under man, but herein also there is a hint of the victory over the one who had used the animal for his purposes. The arch-foe of man is brought to the fore in that God speaks of 'thy head,' and 'thou shalt bruise.' There is a certain solidarity in the kingdom of evil, and that solidarity appears in that the kingdom of evil is here hidden, as it were, behind its head. In the ensuing enmity and conflict, it is not merely the seed of the serpent which will be wounded, nor is it merely from that kingdom that a bruise will be inflicted upon the seed of the woman. Rather, it is the head of that kingdom himself who is brought to the fore and the kingdom is as it were hidden behind him. Here is to be a decisive victory. Not merely will the kingdom over which the evil one rules be defeated, but the very head of that kingdom will receive the capital blow.

We must look again, however, at the striking phrase, 'the seed of the woman.' Here too there is solidarity. If this phrase includes the entirety of humanity, does it not follow that therein included are both those whom God will save and those whom He will not save? Does not the phrase then embrace both the good and the evil, the righteous and the unrighteous? This is so, and we believe that it is so for a purpose. Even here in this first promise we learn that God deals with the world. His salvation is directed, not merely toward individual men and women but toward the seed of the woman, and it is that seed which He saves.

If then the 'seed of the woman' refers to the entirety of the human race and is not a specific prophecy of a personal Messiah, is there no reference at all to Christ? In the year 1951 there appeared, written in German, a valuable commentary upon the first eleven chapters of Genesis. This commentary was valuable, among other reasons, for the faithfulness which it exhibited to the Bible as the Word of God. The author, who passed away recently, was Karlheinz Rabast, a pastor at the Martin Luther Church in Dresden. That such a promising man should be taken from this life is a blow indeed to solid believing Old Testament studies. Yet we may ever be grateful to God that Rabast wrote his commentary on the early chapters of the first book of the Bible.

In this commentary he makes the following interesting remark. 'The seed of the woman is first of all meant in a more general sense; but it has its ultimate and deepest meaning in that it refers to the Virgin Mary and her Seed, Christ.'

What shall we say to this striking comment? It would seem that Rabast has uttered something that is essentially true. We are unable to agree that there is a reference to the Virgin Mary, although some Roman Catholic expositors believe that such is the case. That there is a reference to Christ, however, is not to be rejected. It is true that the prophecy is uttered in general terms, and its primary meaning is that the human race is to be victorious over the serpent. Nevertheless, it is also true that the way in which man will vanquish Satan is that there will be born of woman One, even Jesus Christ, who will obtain the victory. In this sense, this is a prophecy of Christ, and deserves to be known as the Protevangelium. The Bible does not say that the descendants of Adam will overcome, but the seed of the woman. And perhaps it is of note to realize that the word 'seed' is in the singular. It is the seed of the woman as comprehended in the Redeemer that will deliver the fatal blow. We are not willing therefore, to reject offhand, the emphasis that Rabast brings, even though we cannot agree with all that he says.

With evident allusion to this passage Paul declares: 'And the God of peace shall bruise Satan under your feet shortly. The grace of our Lord Jesus Christ be with you. Amen' (Romans 16:20). Satan is to be bruised! It is a remarkable, almost unbelievable truth. God will not allow man to perish but is determined to save him. And with this verse we are introduced to the plan of salvation. Much is still dark: we do not have the clear light of day that the New Testament brings. Even from this verse, however, we learn that God is taking the initiative. He will do for man what man cannot do for himself. He will introduce enmity and the woman's seed will deliver a blow that will destroy the evil one. In this verse there does shine through, and that very clearly, the grace of a Redeemer God.

16. Unto the woman he said: Causing to be great I shall cause to be great thy sorrow and thy conception; in sorrow thou shalt bring forth sons, and unto thy husband will be thy desire, and he will rule over thee.

W̲ITH verse fifteen the rays of sunshine appear. In cursing the serpent God is preparing the way for an announcement of blessing for mankind. Here begins that long line of prophecy which finally culminates in the appearance upon earth of the One who is the true prophet, priest and king. The stream of prophecy begins at this source or fountain head, and from this mother prophecy flows with every increasing fullness until it has accomplished its goal. In the deepest and fullest sense this prophecy of redemption found its fulfilment when the eternal Son of God died upon Golgotha and so bruised the serpent's head.

Although the grace of God is shown in the warfare which is to extend until the Seed of the woman delivers the decisive destructive blow, nevertheless, God manifests His justice also in that the woman is punished. Turning from the serpent, God addresses the woman. Indeed, the order of those addressed is quite striking.

MAN***WOMAN***SERPENT***WOMAN***MAN

No curse, however, is pronounced upon either the

woman or the man. To Satan God had directed a curse, but not to mankind. There are indeed, words of reproof, and these are well deserved, but how gentle they are in comparison with what God spoke to the Tempter! And it is well to note that only after God had made a declaration of salvation, does He rebuke the woman and the man.

In the translation we have tried to bring out the exact force of the Hebrew words. The verbal forms are causative in nature, and we may best render them, 'causing to be great, I shall cause to be great.' At first sight this appears to be a strange idiom, but what it means is that God will most surely make the sorrow and conception of the woman to be great. Although death has come upon man, nevertheless, the human race will still be able to propagate itself. From eternal death there will be deliverance, to be sure, but the fact of physical death has not been removed, and although man will continue to exist upon earth until physical death claims him, nevertheless, his life will be one of sorrow.

With respect to the woman, her sexual life is to be one of sorrow. Out of a desire for earthly enjoyment and sensual pleasure, Eve had broken the commands of God. She therefore is to be punished with the sorrows and pains of pregnancy and childbirth. We may note that the Hebrew word for 'sorrow' by its very sound calls to mind the word for 'tree.' Inasmuch as Eve partook of the forbidden tree ('etz), she is now to discover that her 'sorrow' ('itzyzᵉbonek) will be multiplied. She will be able to propagate the race, so God had just promised, but her life will be one in which this very function of reproduction will remind her of her fall and disobedience.

What however, is meant by this expression, 'thy sorrow'? It would seem to have particular reference to the sorrows that characterize the woman's life. Perhaps those students of Scripture are correct who assert that there was an enfeebling of her body which resulted in a disturbance of the relation between body and soul. Perhaps, too, this sorrow is primarily to be understood in connection with the sexual life of the woman. In connection with this word there is another, namely, 'thy conception,' and this would seem first of all to refer to the pain and discomfort which accompanies pregnancy. Indeed, a certain emphasis falls upon the words 'thy conception,' which we may bring out by rendering 'thy sorrow and in particular thy conception.'

For woman the bearing of children is to be a difficulty. Her conception is not what she might have desired it to be, and not what God had originally designed for her. It was the divine plan that man should be fruitful and multiply and fill the earth. Eve, however, had disobeyed God and sought for enjoyment contrary to God's law. She therefore will be punished in her sexual life, for not only will her pregnancy be unpleasant, but her entire life. The pains which will come to her will threaten her own life, she will go down to the very gate of death before her children come into the world, and throughout the remainder of her life she will be reminded by sorrow that her life is not filled with the enjoyment which she had once erroneously believed would be hers.

Is it then wrong to seek to alleviate the pain of woman in childbearing? What shall be said to those who assert that inasmuch as the divine declaration is that woman will bring forth children in sorrow, it is wrong to seek to change this fact by any means whatever? Such pain, so it is argued, should not be alleviated. With this type of reasoning, we for our part have no sympathy, for it appears to us to misunderstand the language of the Scripture.

All suffering and sickness are the result of sin. The Bible makes it clear that the profession of medicine is an honourable one. Jesus Christ Himself is known as the good Physician. Hence, any method that is not in itself morally wrong may be employed to alleviate the suffering of the woman in childbirth and indeed in her entire sexual life. It will be impossible, however, to eradicate completely the sorrow which the woman must undergo. If woman's sorrow can somewhat be mitigated, and the pain of her conception lessened, then certainly such should be done. This is not to go contrary to God's will, but is to use means of medicine which God Himself has given in order that suffering may be alleviated.

Another remark is in order. Weak as she is, the woman is in need of all the comfort and understanding that her husband can give to her. It may be true that the sexes never fully understand one another, but there is no excuse for the callousness and brutality that some men exhibit toward their wives. The Christian husband must be the understanding husband; he must remember that his wife is living a life in which sorrow, pain and suffering will play a large role. From the effect of the fall she cannot free herself, and the husband, if he is truly to be a husband, must turn toward her in sympathy and love. Affection and tenderness must characterize his attitude toward his wife, if he is to show the Christian compassion and concern that she needs.

What however is the meaning of the last phrase of the verse, 'Unto thy husband shall be thy desire?' What Adam had said about his wife, even though he was not gallant in asserting it, was nevertheless true. She had given to him of the fruit and he ate. In this transaction Eve had taken the lead. It may well be that inasmuch as she had not received a direct command from God, the serpent had approached her. Whether this be the case or not, the woman did lead her husband into sin. She did give to him of the forbidden fruit. In the divinely-imposed arrangement the woman was to occupy a certain position of subordination in that she was to be a help to her husband. In the Lord she was to follow his lead and to aid him as he faced the world. In the temptation and fall, however, she abandoned this subordinate role and sought to assume a position of leadership. Thus she raised herself above the man, emancipating herself from him, and in addition she led him into sin.

By her very nature the woman reaches her supreme position as woman when in the divinely-intended sense she is subordinate to the husband and aids him in his leading. Sin breaks this divine institution, and unhappiness in the married estate flows from an abandonment of what God had intended. When fallen woman seeks to be the equal of man, she does not attain the happiness which she thinks to find. Only in the role of a wife who seeks truly to be a help to her husband does the woman properly fulfil her role.

As we examine the language of the Lord, we note that

it is capable of two interpretations. First of all, however, it is well to compare it with the similar language in Genesis 4:7. In that verse we read, 'and his desire is unto thee.' The meaning in this context of the fourth chapter is that what sin desires is what Cain will carry out. His desire is unto Cain in the sense that Cain is a slave thereto, and must perform whatever sin's desire may be. In the present verse we may render, 'and unto thy husband is thy desire.' It is obvious that the meaning here is the reverse of what it was in the fourth chapter. Is it not clear that in this third chapter the meaning cannot be that the desire of the woman is unto the husband so that he must do what she wishes? Is it not clear that the woman is not here pictured as a despot who compels the man to do the thing that she desires? Plainly this is not the meaning of the text.

Two possibilities seem to be open. On the one hand the verse may mean that the desire of the woman will be subject unto her husband and he will rule over her. *Her* desire, whatever it may be, will not be her own. She cannot do what she wishes, for her husband rules over her like a despot and whatever she wishes is subject to his will.

Another interpretation is that the woman will have a longing and yearning for her husband. Instead of that yearning, so strong that it practically borders on disease, the husband will rule over the woman. Which of these two positions is the correct one? To decide is difficult but, in the light of Genesis 4:7 we incline to the view that the language here refers to the will of the woman being brought into subjection to that of her husband. Between the two positions, there is really not an essential difference.

In the language of the Lord the words 'thy husband' receive a position of emphasis, as they stand first in the clause, 'Unto thy husband is thy desire.' Like her husband the woman also will have desires, but these will be subjected to him. Emancipation of women is an illusion; woman cannot free herself. She is not the equal of the man; only before God is she equal. The tragedy is that her husband will now rule over her. She had sought to rule him in giving to him of the forbidden fruit, but now he will rule over her.

Although there was an original divinely-planned subordination for the woman this was to be a blessing for her. The man was to be her head in the sense that he loved her with a love in which no sin was mixed. He was to love her as he loved himself, and no blot of evil would mar the relationship. All was now changed, for the fall had taken place. Instead of the mild and tender love of Eden, the husband would now domineer over his wife. Over her he would become a despot. In many parts of the world the role of woman has been reduced to that of virtual slavery. Only the Gospel of Jesus Christ has brought a genuine and blessed amelioration of the position of womankind in this fallen world.

'He will rule over thee.' In the light of this strong statement we can the better understand the injunctions of the New Testament. Christian husbands are not to domineer over their wives and relegate them to a position of abject obedience and servitude. Rather they are to love their wives, even as Christ loved the Church and gave Himself for it. Their love to the wife is to be the same as the love of their own body. Statements such as these are strong, indeed, but they are needed. The Christian husband must show that he has been redeemed, and that the right to enter Paradise again has been obtained for him by Christ. No spirit of cruel and selfish domination is to guide him, but such a love for the wife as will exhibit a true concern for her well being and comfort. He must realize that she is suffering in accordance with the words which the Lord has here spoken, and so must exhibit toward her the tenderness of the love which the Bridegroom of the Church has manifested toward His Bride, the Church.

17. And to Adam he said, Because thou hast hearkened to the voice of thy wife, and thou didst eat from the tree which I commanded thee, saying, Thou shalt not eat from it, cursed is the ground for thy sake; in sorrow thou shalt eat it all the days of thy life.

FROM the woman God turns to the man. In the Hebrew language the word for man which has been used throughout this chapter is ADAM. Up until this point the word has always appeared with the definite article, 'the man,' and in the translation we have sought to bring this out. Here, however, the word does not have the definite article, but appears simply as ADAM, and thus is used as a proper name. Thus, God does not speak to the man, but to ADAM, the individual. In hearkening to the voice of his wife Adam had forfeited his position as the crown of creation and the head of the wife, and had placed himself into the subordinate position which belonged to the woman. Instead of showing her the way in which she should walk, he had yielded to her direction and sinned against God. Furthermore, he had listened to her when she was deceived by the serpent. Hence, Adam has abandoned his place of superiority over the creatures.

A second ground for punishment appears in the simple words, 'and thou hast eaten.' In this eating, Adam had not merely forfeited his position of superiority over the creatures but had deliberately disobeyed God, seeking to place himself above God. One who had done these things no longer deserved to live. To him there could be nought but the punishment of death.

In a forceful way the Scripture brings out the sadness of the whole situation. Not only had Adam eaten, but he had eaten from the tree 'which I commanded thee, saying, thou shalt not eat from it.' Adam's act was not one of ignorance. Well did he know that God had forbidden to him the fruit of this particular tree. Despite God's command, he had disobeyed. It is folly to speak of men loving God, when their hearts are inclined to the evil. Knowing full well what God desired of him, Adam chose to do the opposite. Better to hearken to the voice of a deceived woman than to listen to the command of a loving and all wise God! Such is the perversity of sin and such the travesty which it makes of reasoning.

So serious was man's transgression that on account of him the ground is cursed. Yet how can ground be cursed? Ground is something inanimate and not responsible. How is it possible for a curse to be placed upon it? What is meant of course is that the curse upon the ground is with respect to man, so that the one who will feel the effects of the curse is not the ground, inasmuch as the ground is insensible and without life, but man himself. Because of man the curse is pronounced upon the ground. Indeed, the two Hebrew words, ADAM (man) and ADAMAH (ground) show the close relationship between the two.

Although the man himself is not cursed, the ground through him receives that curse, and thus the curse reaches him. A striking difference appears between the manner in which the curse affects woman and that in which it affects man. It strikes the woman in the very depth and heart of her being, bringing her down to the door of death. It strikes the man in that it affects the basis or foundation from which he must derive his substance. Thus, the punishment is aimed as it were at life itself, for he who would exalt himself above God must become subject to death.

Man is of the earth, earthy, but through sin a disturbance in his relationship to the ground enters in. Instead of a friendly earth, a curse now spreads out over the ground and man stands as it were upon enemy soil.

Is it not apparent that sin disturbs and disrupts all normal relationships? In the original creation God had ordained a harmonious relationship among all His creatures and also between Himself and them. No longer, however, does this relationship obtain. In seeking to rise above God man had destroyed that relationship. He now stands at enmity with God, and inasmuch as God is just, He must punish man. Furthermore an estrangement even sets in between the man and the woman as would appear from the crudity of Adam in blaming his wife for his own act. And between man and the earth a rupture, as it were, appears. Satan delights in disorder. Sin does not lead to freedom of expression but only to confusion and death.

Adam is to eat of the ground. It will not deny him its produce, but his eating will be in sorrow. Again, in the very word, 'sorrow' ('*itztzabon*) we are reminded of the word '*etz* (tree). No longer will the earth produce with the ease that was characteristic of Eden. Before the fall, when all became perverted, and order was changed to disorder, the ground brought forth abundantly, and to till the soil and keep the garden was a delight, for the curse of sin was not present. Now all has been changed; toil is a labour and a burden; only in sorrow does the earth give her yield to man.

Is then work a curse in itself? Obviously such is not the case. Adam had been placed in the garden for a specific purpose. 'And he placed him in the garden of Eden to work it and to keep it' (Genesis 2:15b). In these words there is a responsibility placed upon Adam. He has a task to perform, and for the faithful discharge of that task is to answer to God. Man was not created an irresponsible creature as would seem to be the case were no responsibility placed upon him. In the goodness of God, a definite task was given, and the performance of this task would have been man's highest enjoyment for in carrying it out he would wholeheartedly be labouring for the glory of the Creator whom he loved.

Work in itself is surely no curse. The working of the ground of Eden would have been a blessing, but now that same ground will reluctantly, as it were, yield to man its produce. Happy is that man today whose life consists in doing the work in which his heart is! How few there are that have found such occupation! How many to whom daily work is burdensome, almost cruel toil! Even at best however, our work is filled with fatigue, and enjoy it as we may, we do not enjoy it perfectly.

How long will such a condition continue? The answer is given succinctly, 'All the days of thy life.' The language implies that there will be an end to man's life. He is not to remain upon this earth forever. Death will come, for he is already in its power. Yet man does not immediately die. In permitting him to live God has not relented from the purpose expressed in 2:17. The penalty of death must fall. The mercy and goodness of God are seen, however, in that man is not immediately cast into eternal punishment and death but that the mercy of salvation is announced to him.

18. And thorn and thistle will it cause to sprout to thee, and thou shalt eat the herb of the field.

Not willingly and freely will the earth produce the food which will sustain man and keep him in life. Instead it will bring forth thorns and thistles which will choke out the sustenance-producing plants. At best toil is to be a constant struggle for existence, a painful, death-bringing labour. The principle herein taught is that all labour will be difficult, but this principle is illustrated by that labour which has to do with tilling the soil. It would seem therefore, that the text suggests that man must engage in a severe struggle for his own existence. He will till the soil, but it will send forth thorns and thistles.

In contrast to the trees of the garden, man will simply eat the herb of the ground. It has been suggested that we really find in the words of the curse a reflection upon two different manners of life. One of these has in mind the peasant, known in Egypt as the Fellaheen, who leads an agricultural life. The other refers to the Bedouin who wanders about in the steppes. The present verse, with its emphasis upon thorns and thistles and the herbs of the ground is said to point to this latter type of life. The wanderer leads a beggarly existence, eating what meagre food he can find. On the other hand, the references to toiling, it is said, point more to the life of the farmer. Here were originally two independent traditions, which in the course of time have become fused. But is this really a satisfactory explanation of what we have before us? We must remember that we are living in a day when some people have only to look at the Old Testament to cry 'tradition' or 'saga'. Having rejected the Bible as the special revelation from God which it is (2 Timothy 3:16) they seek to account for it as a merely human production. And this is not easy to do. In fact it is impossible. The history of man's attempts to explain the Bible as only a human work is kaleidoscopic in nature. One view supplants another with remarkable rapidity.

If, however, we assert that everything in the Old Testament goes back to times of hoary antiquity, have we really explained anything? Is the Old Testament, and in particular this chapter, just an old tradition which in one form or another was handed down from generation to generation? Is it merely man's attempt to find the answers to a number of problems? If that is all it is, why pay particular attention to it? If the Bible is only the work of man, it is only the work of man, and there is no reason why we should pay more attention to its thoughts than to those of the Greeks.

What we have here, however, are not ancient traditions, but the revelation of God, and that revelation points out to man how his life upon earth will be miserable and wretched and also how difficult his toil will be. As it stands, the Bible at this point exhibits a striking unity; why break it up? Why look for two old traditions which represent two different backgrounds when actually what is said is a harmonious unity?

19. In the sweat of thy nostrils thou shalt eat bread until thy returning unto the ground, for from it thou wast taken, for dust art thou and unto dust thou shalt return.

In the translation we have purposely brought out the force of the Hebrew original. In speaking of the nostrils the Hebrew means the countenance, for the nostrils are the most prominent part of the face. Hard labour will produce sweat, and so man will toil to eat bread. The word 'bread' probably refers, not to food in general, but to food that is produced from the ground. Job declares (28:5) that 'As for the earth, out of it cometh bread: and under it is turned up as it were fire,' and the Psalmist (104:14) says, 'He causeth the grass to grow for the cattle, and herb for the service of man: that he may bring forth food out of the earth'. In this passage from the Psalm the word rendered 'food' is in the Hebrew original 'bread.'

Again an emphasis upon death. Having been formed of the dust of the ground man is to return to that dust. Man had wanted to be like God, but he is only dust. Herein is the culmination of the threat 'thou shalt surely die.' As soon as man had disobeyed God he became mortal. The power of death came over him and the germ of death entered his nature. He was separated from God and in the throes of spiritual, eternal death. The germ must ripen, and when it does man's body will be dissolved and return to the dust from which he was taken. We must note the force of the word 'till'. It is not used in a chronological sense, as though merely to teach that man would eat bread until his return to the dust. Rather, it is emphatic and climactic in force. Man is to eat bread and this eating of bread as a result of hard toil will culminate in death. Man is the loser in his struggle with the ground, for, as it were, the ground will at last overcome him. Death is not the natural end for man, but a tragic punishment for his disobedience.

*20. And Adam called the name of his
wife Eve, for she was the mother
of all living.*

BETWEEN verses nineteen and twenty a sharp contrast appears. Man is dust, yet he calls his wife the mother of all living. Why does the Scripture assert that man is dust? Is this a way of saying that man now passes into non-being? Does the Bible know nothing of a life everlasting? These are questions which some wish to answer in the affirmative. Can they however, be so answered? We think not. In his designation of the woman as Eve, the mother of all living, Adam reveals his belief that life will continue to flow from her. Furthermore, the promise which has just been enunciated in verse fifteen is truly a Protevangelium. It does present a declaration of victory over the serpent, and victory over the serpent involves life in contrast to death. By disobedience to God man did indeed fall into a state of death, but through the blow to be struck by the seed of the woman, he is to be delivered and deliverance points to life. Hence, in the light of these considerations we may be sure that although there is at this point no explicit statement of everlasting life, nevertheless, the Bible is showing that death will not conquer man. Well will it be if we note also the language of the twenty second verse, 'And now, lest he stretch forth his hand and eat, and live forever.' In this language there is a reference to living forever which is quite opposed to the idea that the Bible pictures death as a passing into non-being.

In speaking of man as dust, then, the Bible does not wish to assert that he will cease to exist. Nor does it intend us to understand that man is nothing more than dust. It is to the body of man that reference is particularly made. One who reads the Hebrew will not fail to notice the word-play between man (ADAM) and ground (ADAMAH). It is now a sad connection. God formed man's body dust from the ground. Man sought to exalt himself above God. Yet he is but dust. Instead of the exalted height of heaven, he must now return unto the dust for from this dust he was taken.'

Some seem to think that between verses nineteen and twenty there is a break, but is this really the case? Is there not rather a remarkable connection which brings to the fore a striking contrast. Because of his sin man's body will return to the dust, for it is of the dust, but man himself will not die. He will continue to live. Responding to God's declaration of salvation, man engages in an act of faith. Believing that he will live he calls his wife's name Eve. He himself possessed a name, even MAN, for the Hebrew word for man and Adam is one and the same. Eve however, possessed no name, and it was necessary that she be given a name commensurate with her nature and position.

In trust upon God's promise Adam therefore names her Eve. The word means 'she who gives life.' It is an interesting word. In the Hebrew we would pronounce it *Hawwah*. Note that the second consonant of the word is doubled. In the Semitic languages words whose second consonant is doubled, and which have two *a* vowels indicate one who customarily or habitually performs a certain action. A *naggar*, for example, is a carpenter, one who is engaged in the trade of carpentry. So also an *Hawwah* is one who is engaged in the work of giving life. This is a strong way of asserting that life will surely come from Eve. Death is cheated of its prey, for God has intervened.

There is nothing in this name itself which suggests or presupposes that Eve has already borne children, and attempts to read such a meaning into the word are without justification. Equally unfounded and unwarranted are attempts to connect the word Eve with the Aramaic *hewya* which means serpent. Those who attempt to make such a connection are apparently desirous of reading into the text thoughts about a serpent deity. But all such efforts are without justification.

What about those who say that here is a second naming of the woman? Was she not already named in the previous chapter (verse 23) when Adam said, 'she shall be called Woman?' For our part we can see no merit in such an interpretation. At the creation of woman, Adam does not give her a name as an individual, but merely expresses recognition of her nature as woman. In the present verse, on the contrary, Adam is speaking not of womankind as such, but of his wife alone. She is now named Eve, and this is the first time in the Bible that she as an individual receives a name.

At the close of the verse a reason is assigned why Eve
was so named. Are these words of the reason the words
of Adam himself, or are they rather an insertion by Moses,
the author of the Pentateuch? In all probability the latter
is correct. There was good reason for naming his wife
Eve, for she was the mother of all living. These words of
explanation sound as though they were spoken at a time
when there were many living and all mankind could
trace itself back to Eve as its mother. She is the life-giver
par excellence, for she is the mother of all who live. As
over against the background of death brought about by
man's sin, this verse stresses the thought of life. Life is
given and received in faith, for God has acted and announced that there will be deliverance.

21. Unto Adam also and to his wife did the Lord God make coats of skin and he clothed them.

*F*OLLOWING Adam's act of faith, God performed one of grace. Man is not to stand naked before God but is to be clothed. What, however, does this mean? Does God respect man in his shame, and does man now stand before God in the relationship of religion? Sometimes an affirmative answer is given to these questions. Religion, it has been said, is man's sense of shame in the presence of God and his attempt to clothe himself before Him. Is this, however, what we have here, or is not the meaning of the action of God far more profound? Indeed, it is; man's attempt to clothe himself is not necessarily praiseworthy; it is even rejected by God. Nor do we really get to the heart of the matter by asserting that God respects man in his nakedness. In his nakedness man is a lost creature, and what awaits him, if nothing is done for him, is that the seed of sin within, which his nakedness represents, will grow and develop until it issues in physical death, and that physical death is but a sign or manifestation of separation from God, the death that is eternal.

Nor do we come to an understanding of the situation by the assumption that there is some tension with verse seven, and that the two verses probably derive from differing circles of tradition. There is rather a perfect agreement with verse seven, and the idea that there are two sources of tradition is completely without support or evidence. In verse seven we read of the futile attempt of fallen man to cover the results of his sin. Clearly such an attempt cannot be accepted by God; man's salvation does not come to him on the basis of human works but only by divine grace. Man cannot be regarded as clothed until he is properly clothed with the clothing provided by God Himself. Hence, there is no tension but only the most perfect harmony between the present verse and verse seven.

To bring the two verses side by side as we have done is nevertheless quite a wholesome thing, for it points out the heart of the matter. And that is that man is not regarded by God as clothed until he is properly clothed. From the present verse we learn that proper clothing comes only from God. And that is a lesson which fallen mankind needs to learn. Men are living under the sway of the great deception, namely, that fallen and sinful man is able to clothe himself. In modern terms, this simply means that man thinks he is able to solve all his problems in his own strength. Is war a threat? He will overcome it and establish a just and lasting peace. Is race tension present? He will pass laws, be they just or otherwise, and so do away with race tension. Is there strife between management and labour? Man will settle the matter, so that there be no more strife. If need be he will use threats and coercion, but he will settle the matter. And is there something wrong with the human heart? No, not really, whatever there is can easily be taken care of. After all, the malady which some call sin is to be attributed to man's environment. Proper housing, proper education, these and the like are what fallen man suggests as the remedy for whatever seems to be amiss. But all of these are simply man's attempts to clothe himself. In the presence of God they must be rejected, for 'it is not by works of righteousness that we have done, but according to his mercy that he hath saved us.' This truth, so clearly enunciated in the New Testament, is also present here in Genesis.

Only God can properly clothe man. If we have learned that truth, we have learned much, and it is that truth which so clearly stands out in this verse. At the same time, it is proper to note what is stated in the New Testament, namely, 'For as many of you as have been baptized into Christ have put on Christ' (Galatians 3:27). To be properly clothed, in the deepest sense, is to be in Christ, for only in Him do we receive that clothing of perfect righteousness which is acceptable with God. True enough, someone may say, but this is New Testament teaching; it is not present here in Genesis. It is wrong to read into the text what is not found there. To which we may heartily agree that it is wrong to read into the text, but are we, at this point, reading into the text, if we find Christ there?

We may perhaps answer the question as follows. Christ is in all the Old Testament, but it is not always possible for us to see Him explicitly in each verse. And there is truly a danger that we try to read Christ into a passage in a way that is not warrantable. Quite possibly the desire to find Christ in the Old Testament, commendable as it is in itself, may lead to a neglecting or slighting of the study of the individual text of the Old Testament. Of that danger we are all too aware. At the same time, we do not properly study any verse of the Bible unless we study it in the light of the context of the whole Scripture, and indeed we do not do justice to it unless we consider all that Scripture has to say about it.

With respect to this verse that we are now considering it is true that what meets us first of all is the fact that only God can provide an acceptable clothing for man. And to have learned that much is to have learned a great deal. We must remember, however, that the Scripture is dealing with something more profound than man's physical clothing. Those interpreters who have seen in this passage nothing more than a statement about man's oldest clothing or that man's cultural achievements are due to God have completely missed the point of the narrative. It is not merely physical nakedness and physical clothing with which the narrative is concerned.

As physical nakedness after the fall becomes a symbol of shame and shame is a sign of man's spiritually fallen nature, so also the clothing of that nakedness has a spiritual import. Man cannot clothe his nakedness, for man cannot deliver himself from the spiritual bondage into which sin has plunged him. To be properly clothed, he must possess a clothing that is acceptable with God, and such clothing must be furnished him by God. When he is properly clothed God will look upon him with favour, regarding him as standing in a right relationship with Himself. The mere skins of animals, however, in themselves cannot clothe the sinful condition of man; they cannot hide his nakedness. Only the righteousness of Christ can do that. If man therefore, is properly clothed he is in Christ. God would behold him properly clothed, clothed with a righteousness which is not his own, but the righteousness of another. God would behold man clothed in the righteousness of Jesus Christ. No, we have not read into the text when we see Christ here, for only in Christ is man properly clothed.

Only that principle of Biblical interpretation is legitimate which accepts the whole Bible as the Word of God and brings to bear upon any subject all that the Bible has to say about it. This method of study is what is called 'systematic theology,' and its significance cannot be overrated. We simply do not have all the truth that God wants us to have on any subject unless we consider everything that He has said about that subject.

Why, however, did the Lord God take the skins of animals? Was it that these in themselves were better and more suitable than the leaves of the fig tree? This question is perhaps not as easy to answer as at first sight might seem to be the case. It has been suggested of course, that the skins of animals point to the fact that blood has been shed, and of course, without the shedding of blood there is no remission. Possibly this is the reason why animal lives were taken, but of this we cannot be sure. What seems to stand out most clearly is the fact that God alone must decide what clothing is suitable for man, and it may be, that in order to make the contrast stronger, inasmuch as man had chosen the leaves of the fig tree, God chose the skins of animals.

Furthermore, this act of God did show to man that there was a distinction between man and the animals. Man was sovereign over the animals and he might use them, even taking their lives, when this was necessary for his own need and preservation. It would also appear that this act of God in the taking of animal life laid the foundation for animal sacrifice. More than that it does not seem permissible to assert.

There is a danger that an over-literal interpretation may tend to make this verse appear ludicrous. We are not necessarily to understand that in providing clothing for man God actually used His own fingers to sew this clothing together. Indeed we are not told precisely how God provided this clothing. What is important is that the clothing is a gift from Him. It was His work, although how the actual preparation was carried out we do not know. Possibly, God may have given to man the necessary directions for sewing the skins together. Man stands alone in need of clothing, and God in His goodness provides for that need of man.

22. And the Lord God said, Behold!
the man is become as one of us, to know
good and evil: and now, lest he put forth
his hand, and take also of the tree of life,
and eat, and live forever.

W HAT now is the condition of the man whom God has clothed? Is he in such a condition that all is well and he may have free access to the tree of life in the garden? God speaks concerning him, and only in the light of God's pronouncement can we understand why God drives him from the garden. 'The man has now become as one of us.' In themselves these words are simple, but many are the interpretations which have been imposed upon them. Luther thought that the Lord was speaking ironically, as though to mock at the idea that man could be like Himself. Such, irony, however, which would be at the expense of one who had incurred God's displeasure and was about to be banished from the garden, is certainly out of place. It might befit Satan, but not the Lord of mercy. Another view is that there is no point of comparison between man and the Lord, inasmuch as the plural is used 'like one of us'. The comparison rather is between man and the gods. Man has ceased to understand himself as a creature and no longer permits himself to obey but rather follows his own autonomous willing and knowing. And yet another interpretation is that man, like the angelic beings who inhabit the heavenly court has now become a responsible being. He is sinful, however, and must not forever possess attributes which he will misuse.

All of these views are interesting, but are they correct? For our part, we believe that they are not, and the point at which they all (with the exception of Martin Luther's view) fail, is that they have not done justice to the words 'one of us.' What then do these words mean? They certainly do not mean that the Lord is only one of many gods. That would be polytheism, and the Old Testament consistently rejects anything that even remotely resembles polytheism. In answer to this, however, it is said that what we have here in the third chapter of Genesis is a composite of old traditions which go back to a very early time. In these old traditions there may very well have been snatches of polytheistic conceptions. To this we would reply that there is no evidence whatever, despite some of the latest commentaries on Genesis, that the third chapter or that this verse of the third chapter are composites of old traditions. And even if they had been such composites, it is most unlikely that the supposed editor, a man who was eager to defend the religion of Jehovah whose basic tenet was that there is but one God, would have permitted a remnant of polytheism to creep in. For our part we believe that this verse, and indeed the entire chapter, is the revealed Word of God. When God revealed it for the first time to man, and how God the Holy Spirit superintended the human writer of this chapter, we do not know. We are convinced, however, that there is no evidence to support the position that the chapter consists of ancient human traditions, handed down from time immemorial. One is tempted to ask those who constantly make such an assertion to produce a bit of evidence in support of their dogmatic claim.

If then we accept the third chapter of Genesis as the Word of God, a part of that 'all Scripture' which has been God breathed, how are we to interpret these difficult words? If they do not point to polytheism, what do they mean? One very ancient answer is that they refer to the divine court. This divine court, it is said, consists of angelic beings, who work with the Lord. Here, then, God is including this court, and when he asserts that the man 'has become as one of us,' He means that the man has become as one of His own heavenly court. The man is still a creature, but he has become like creatures who go to make up God's court. In the word 'us,' then, God is including the members of His heavenly court.

This is very interesting, but it does not fit well into the context. For one thing, why should God object merely because the man had become like one of the members of the heavenly court? It must be remembered that the specific point in which the likeness is found is that of knowing good and evil. If then, like members of the heavenly court, the man also knows good and evil, why on that account alone, should he be banished from the garden? Furthermore, throughout this chapter the contrast has been between God on the one hand and man on the other. The promise which the tempter had held out to the woman was that if she partook of the forbidden tree she would be like God. It was the desire to be like God that influenced the woman. If, now, as a result of eating the forbidden fruit, man and woman are only like heavenly beings and not like God, it seems strange that on that account they would be driven from the garden. This interpretation does not fit in well with the whole context of the chapter.

It would seem then that the word 'us' must refer to God Himself, and that God is here declaring that man has now become like Him, in that he knows good and evil. If this is the case, why is the plural used? Why does not the Lord simply say that the man has become like Me? The plural is not a plural of majesty, but, like the similar plural of Genesis 1:26 (let us make man in our image) indicates that in the Speaker there is a plurality of persons. Those fathers of the church who saw in these words an adumbration of the doctrine of the Trinity had a deep and penetrating insight. Only this interpretation does justice to the full and deep meaning of the words. Something more profound is being uttered here than the weak conception that man has become like a higher creature. What the Lord is saying is that man has become like God Himself in that he knows good and evil. It is for this reason that he cannot stay in the garden longer. He must be expelled. Man now possesses the knowledge of good and evil, but he misinterprets this knowledge; he leans toward the evil and hates the good. Good and evil he knows from the standpoint of the sinner. He had sought to be like God; like God he had become, but in what a perverted sense! He is now the slave of evil. God is good and hates the evil. Man is evil and hates the good. The possession of this knowledge is made the ground for the action about to be taken by God.

And action must be taken. There is danger that the

man now put forth his hand and take of the fruit of the tree of life and eat and live forever. This must not happen, but why must it not happen? To answer these questions we must consider the meaning of the tree of life, which now for the first time is mentioned in this chapter. This fact has led some to question the unity of the narrative. Indeed, they think that there are contradictions. In chapter two, verse nine, it is stated that the tree of life is in the midst of the garden, but in the third chapter it is the tree of the knowledge of good and evil which is in the midst of the garden. Here, it is asserted, there is a glaring contradiction. As we have seen, some seek to avoid this difficulty by maintaining that there is but one tree, and that this tree is known by the two designations. The narrative in chapter three, however, makes it clear that this interpretation cannot be accepted.

For our part we are unable to see any contradiction here. Only by pressing the language in an unnatural sense, can one discover a contradiction. What is meant by the midst of the garden? Does it mean the precise centre, and if it does, how big is the centre? Is it one inch square, or is it a foot square? What right do we have to make the language of Scripture appear ludicrous? Why may not both trees have been in the midst of the garden? Like our English word 'midst,' the Hebrew word also is not a precise mathematical term. It means about what our English word means. Does it designate so small an area that there is room for only one tree? Cannot two trees be said to be in the midst of the garden, or has modern scholarship lost its sense of balance?

In chapter two the tree of life is mentioned first and is

described as being in the midst of the garden. There is a reason for this. The tree is of sacramental nature and teaches that life comes from God and that man's religion is to be God-centred. The garden is the abode which God prepared for man, and in the centre of that abode, is God Himself. Man's being is to be centred about God. All his life is to be devoted to glorifying God and enjoying Him. God-centred religion is represented by the tree which is in the midst of the garden, and this tree is associated with that higher, unchangeable and eternal life which will belong to man if he overcomes in the probation. 'To him that overcometh will I give to eat of the tree of life, which is in the midst of the paradise of God' (Revelation 2:7). Having successfully passed the probation man will be entitled to partake of the tree of life. At the very out-set, then, we learn that this tree is in the midst of the garden. Almost casually the author mentions the tree of the knowledge of good and evil. In verse seventeen of chapter two, however, attention is directed to the tree of the knowledge of good and evil. By refusing to eat of this tree, and so obeying God, man will have successfully passed the probation, and will then be entitled to partake of the tree of life. Only in the third chapter, however, do we learn that the tree of the knowledge of good and evil was also in the midst of the garden.

Having failed the probation man is no longer entitled to partake of the tree of life. Those interpretations which think that we have here an ancient tradition going back to a belief in magical trees whose fruit provides immor-tality, have not really understood the nature of the third chapter of Genesis. There was no magic quality in the fruit of the tree of life, any more than there was in the fruit of the tree of the knowledge of good and evil.

The tree has sacramental significance. It signifies life, the life that comes from God. Only he may partake of that tree who has the right thereto. Had Adam now eaten of this tree, he would have taken something that did not belong to him. The very act of partaking would have been stealing. To have eaten, we may suppose, would have brought him into an estate of everlasting living, from which there could have been no deliverance. To live forever when one is in the power of sin and death is not the eternal life that God gives to those who believe on Him, but is rather an everlasting death. From this estate there could be no deliverance, no freedom, but only the bondage of life in death. To drive man from the garden, then, was an act of punishment, but it was also an act of kindness, for man must be kept from the tree of life until there come a man who should earn the right for Adam to partake thereof. To live forever in a state of sin would be a curse, not a blessing. God's action, therefore, is not prompted from motives of envy, but rather from love to fallen man and from a desire ultimately to save him.

23. *Therefore the Lord God sent him forth from the garden of Eden, to till the ground from whence he was taken.*

WHAT was the conclusion of God's deliberation? We expect some such words as, 'I shall drive him forth from the garden.' Abruptly, however, the language of the Lord is broken, and the Scripture passes from God's words to God's action. In this very abruptness we see the forcefulness of the narrative. There is no need that we be told what God said, for what God does is sufficient. In order that the tragic condition mentioned in the preceding verse might not come to pass, God expelled man from the garden.

Very interesting is the statement of man's expulsion. In this verse a verb is used which simply means that God sent the man forth. The verb is general and gives no details as to the manner of the expulsion. What it does point to is the fact that God is in control of the situation. It is God's to decide who may and who may not remain in the garden, and when God decides to drive anyone from the garden, there is no one that can stay His hand.

General as is the statement, it is nevertheless of tremendous significance. When God created man He did not place him in a barren and waste wilderness, but formed for him a place of beauty and delight for his abode. The garden which God planted eastward in Eden was God's garden, and man was placed in that garden as God's guest. Here he was to labour in order that he might thereby glorify the One who had created him. Now, however, all is changed. Now, man no longer may remain in the garden. His life to this point has been characterized by base ingratitude toward the One who had made him and given him the garden. God had placed a probation before him, but he had not passed the test. Such a creature does not deserve to remain in Eden. It is well to think of this when we are tempted to believe that all is right with man. We cannot solve our own problems, and we cannot save ourselves, for we are not worthy to abide in the garden of God. Scripture here recounts a tragic event; God sent man forth from the garden.

Many men have laboured earnestly to expound this portion of the Bible. Much of what they have written is worthwhile and helpful; much, however, is of little merit. One of the most penetrating expositors of the Old Testament was Carl Friedrich Keil. For some twenty-five years Keil taught the Old Testament to theological students at Dorpat. Seeing the influence of rationalistic commentaries in Germany, he left his work of instruction and taking up residence in Leipzig, devoted thirteen years to the preparation of a commentary on the Old Testament which would be written from the viewpoint of one who loved the Old Testament and believed it to be the revealed Word of God. On this third chapter of Genesis Keil has many fine and helpful things to say, and he, perhaps as well as anyone, has characterized this action of the Lord, 'The expulsion from Paradise, therefore, was a punishment inflicted for man's good, intended, while exposing him to temporal death, to preserve him from eternal death.' Even in this act the mercy of God and His concern for mankind appear.

Was man simply thrust forth not knowing where he was to go or why? There was a purpose in the expulsion. He was to till the ground, and in the word which we translate 'till' there is reflection upon the same word that was used in the second chapter when it was stated that man was to till the garden. Actually the word simply means 'to work.' As Adam was originally intended to work the garden of Eden, so now he is to work the ground generally. His labours are not restricted to Eden as originally. Indeed, he will no longer be in Eden. The whole world is before him, and he is to work the ground in order to provide for his living.

We cannot agree with those who think that this account teaches how man left Paradise and became a farmer. It is a mistake, we think, to limit the meaning of the words 'to till' to the work of a farmer. Emphasis falls here upon this one particular work, for it stands in contrast to the work that Adam was to have done in the garden. But there is nothing in the text which excludes other work as well. The meaning is general. From now on, man must provide for himself through work, and that work will be in connection with the ground on which man is to live. Not without purpose does the Scripture add 'from which thou wast taken.' Man is not to forget that he is of the earth, and that his body came from the ground.

24. So he drove out the man: and he placed at the east of the garden of Eden Cherubim, and a flaming sword which turned every way to keep the way of the tree of life.

THIS is no mere repetition of what has already been stated. In verse 23 we had the general statement of Adam's expulsion from Eden; here the details are given. It was not only a sending away; it was a driving forth. Moses uses a verb in the intensive stem to make clear that Adam was actually driven forth from the garden. Not one moment more than necessary is he to remain in the garden. His departure must be with haste. He is now a usurper and has no right to be present in the garden. Hence, God drives him forth. The manner of his expulsion consisted in being driven forth.

Is not this the very essence of death? Had the principle of death not found its rest in the heart of man, man would not have been expelled from Eden. God's word had been true, for in the day of Adam's eating of the forbidden fruit, death did find entrance into his soul. And a creature which is under the dominion and power of death cannot remain in the garden of God where is the tree of life. To God's garden man is from henceforth to be a stranger. Instead he is to go about upon the ground until at last the seed of death matures and breaks forth claiming him for its own. He had been a guest in God's garden; he is now a bondslave of death.

So he is to live his life upon this earth. In vain will he seek to solve his own problems, to bring peace to his warring world, to stamp out the effects of his sin. And what is most tragic, he will not, unless God from on high enlighten him, even understand the nature of his condition. Living in sin and misery, the child of death, he will deceive himself into thinking that his malady is after all nothing more than a question of environment. Let man find proper housing and proper schooling, let him banish ignorance and disease and poverty, and all will be well. Thus man, when he has turned his thought to the conditions in which he finds himself, seeks to discover answers.

But such answers are in vain. The best of housing and schooling and abundance of wealth do not overcome man's condition. What he needs, and what he refuses to believe that he needs, is power from God. Man in the world is lost, in every sense of the word. He looks to himself for help, when the only help that avails is in the name of the Lord who made heaven and earth. Yet he ever keeps up the ghastly fiction. He has created religions many and gods many and all of them have this in common that they look to man for the answer to their problems.

Adam at least, having been expelled from the garden, went forth, under the power of death and yet a child of hope. He knew that from his wife there would be born a deliverer. Imperfectly, it is true, did he understand this truth, but he did at least possess the promise, and it was a promise made by Him that cannot lie. Having had dealings with one who can lie and who did lie, Adam and Eve now have the assurance of One whose Word is truth.

Until the right is obtained for him, there is to be no returning into the garden. At the east of the garden, quite probably at the spot where Adam and his wife took their exit, God caused to dwell the cherubim in order to protect the entrance into the garden. The Bible does not tell us too much about these cherubim. Evidently they do signify the glory of God's own presence, for we read in the Psalm, 'And He rode upon a cherub and did fly, yea He did swoop down upon the wings of the wind' (18:10). The cherubim are also said to surround God's throne (Ezekiel 1:22; Rev. 4:6).

Differing interpretations of the cherubim have been offered, and there is no point in considering them all. Some of the early Church Fathers, for example, thought that they were simply symbolic figures. Others practically identify them with the angels or at least speak of them as angel-like beings. Of course there are those who think that we have to do here with ancient Oriental mythology, and that there is perhaps a reflection upon Babylonian beliefs, suggested for example, by the stone monsters with wings which stand guard over the palace. Then too it has been proposed that they are personifications of the storm cloud whereas the flaming sword is said to be a personification of lightning.

There is not much that can be said. That they were responsible creatures would seem to be the case, for quite possibly their task was to wield the flaming sword. When the Israelites were later commanded to make two of the cherubim for the ark of the covenant, they apparently knew what the figures looked like, inasmuch as no further description of the cherubim is given.

Perhaps too we are justified in assuming that these beings were visible to man. God also placed with the cherubim the flame of a sword which turned constantly as a symbol of the wrath that would be poured out upon the trespasser. The language is interesting and we may render it literally, 'the flame of the sword which turns.' It is the sword, however, and not the flame, which is described as turning. Possibly this was a flame of fire which revealed a revolving sword. At any rate its presence vindicated the cherubim as the watchers of the garden.

How long, it may be asked, did the cherubim and the sword remain in the garden? For that matter, how long did the garden itself continue to exist? Upon questions such as these the Word of God is perfectly silent, and consequently, any speculation upon our part would be futile. It has been held that the garden remained until it was destroyed by the flood. It has also been held that, with the expulsion of Adam, the garden disappeared or was destroyed. There is no evidence, however, to support either of these two positions. When God removed the cherubim and when He caused the garden to disappear we are not told.

Our thoughts from now on are no longer to be occupied with this earthly Paradise. God did not destroy Eden before the eyes of Adam and Eve nor did He take from the tree of life its sacramental significance. Into the garden, however, Adam and Eve are not to return, until there come that Seed of the Woman who will satisfy the divine justice on behalf of all God's own, who by death will abolish death and its power and will in triumph rise from the grave. Then, in the new Jerusalem, because of the Mediator, man will have access to the fruit of the tree of life. Man is banished from the garden in death, but the chapter closes with the word 'life.' That life is one day to be his, even though death has for the time claimed him. Yet even in death, man has the promise of life.

> *'I am a branch in Thee, the Vine,*
> *And hence the comfort borrow*
> *That Thou wilt surely keep me Thine*
> *Through fear and pain and sorrow;*
> *And when I die, I die to Thee,*
> *Thy precious death hath won for me*
> *The life that never endeth.'*

Epilogue

WE leave the chapter with the word LIFE ringing in our ears. And it is well that it should be so. For we are without the garden and when we seek to re-enter there are the cherubim and the flaming sword which turns to keep the way of the tree of life. Adam, according to the New Testament, acted on our behalf, as our representative, and when he sinned, we sinned also in him. Herein is a solidarity, for 'by one man sin entered into the world, and death by sin, and so death passed upon all men, for that all had sinned.'

In the midst of this earthly life we are in death. Nor can we earn for ourselves the right to partake of the tree of life. There is only One, the second Adam, the Lord from heaven, who acted on our behalf, and by one righteous Act has obtained for us the title to eternal life and has rendered satisfaction for the guilt of our sin. As God dealt with us through the first Adam, so also does He deal with the world through the second Adam. In this second Adam there is life and hope and peace. In Him there is a return to the garden. And one day we shall eat of the fruit of the tree of life, for His precious blood has been shed. Only in Him who was dead and liveth for evermore, do we have LIFE.